SAINT LAURENT rive gauche

MW00784899

SAINT LAURENT
rive gauche

ABRAMS
NEW YORK

Fondation
PIERRE BERGÉ
YVES SAINT LAURENT

FASHION REVOLUTION

Foreword by Pierre Bergé

Essays by Jéromine Savignon and Gilles de Bure

YVES SAINT LAURENT VENTURES INTO THE SOCIAL ARENA
Pierre Bergé — 8

THE VOYAGE TO RIVE GAUCHE
Jéromine Savignon — 15

BEAUTY FOR ALL
Gilles de Bure — 147

9.
26.
66

Yves Saint Laurent
announces the opening
of his store Saint Laurent
Rive Gauche, 21 rue de
Tournon, Paris.

YVES SAINT LAURENT VENTURES INTO THE SOCIAL ARENA

In 1966, no one could have predicted that September 26 would become a key date in the history of fashion. On that day, the first Yves Saint Laurent Rive Gauche store opened in Paris. It was the first time a great couturier had designed ready-to-wear and given it as much thought as haute couture. Earlier on, Pierre Cardin had tried making clothes for the Printemps department store, but that attempt wasn't the same and it hadn't panned out.

Today it all seems perfectly natural. We need to remind ourselves that at the time, the great labels did not have outlets all over the world. Boutiques selling Dior, Chanel, Prada, Armani, Gucci, etc., were not the common sights they are today. By opening a boutique separate from his fashion house, Saint Laurent was actually performing a revolutionary act, moving away from aesthetics and venturing into the social arena. It was a manifesto.

"Fashion would be a sad business if all it did was put clothes on rich women." From this observation by Yves Saint Laurent came the whole idea of the Rive Gauche store.

The twentieth century gave rise to many couturiers, some of them very talented designers whose names live on today. We could cite Dior, Balenciaga, Grès, Schiaparelli, Vionnet, Balmain, and Lanvin, among others. All of them, understandably, designed clothes for the "rich women" Saint Laurent referred to. It would never have occurred to them to work for the ordinary woman. Only Chanel took issue with the creative regimen that ignored changes in society and the social role of women. In her own way, she liberated women, and she would probably have gone further if World War II had not intervened.

In the postwar years, Christian Dior dressed women in his New Look.[1] Women were back, as it were, to the distant days when they wore stifling corsets but were proud of their clothing and their elegance. The couturier laid down the law and changed the silhouette year after year, lengthening and shortening hemlines at will.

Fashion is an extraordinary reflection of its time. And sometimes it even leads the way. In the second half of the twentieth century, women moved closer to the forefront. They achieved the right to vote in 1944. Fashion designs could no longer be made against women or for women; they had to be made with women. It was this realization that gave Saint Laurent's talent and intuition its true impetus. He felt more deeply than other couturiers the tremors that were shaking the world. September 1966 was a full twenty months before May 1968, when France's youth took to the streets calling for freedom. Many people were deaf to the signals arriving from all sides, but Yves Saint Laurent understood that an old order was coming to an end, that the familiar codes would soon be replaced by fresh ones, and that a struggle would take place in which women would assert their equal place in society. He wanted to take part in the struggle and, in a modest way, play a role in it.

1. After the rationing of fabric during World War II, the New Look boasted an extravagant quantity of fabric, creating a feminine style distinguished by full skirts and petticoats, as well as fitted jackets and strapless boned tops.

His first decision was to design within the framework of industrial manufacturing. He developed no details or tailoring or finishing that could not be produced in the factory—unlike the designs of haute couture. He confined his creativity to the factory's capabilities. This was one of his great strengths.

When we opened the store, we wanted it to be somewhere other than at the fashion house. We opted for the Left Bank in Paris, and we called the store "Rive Gauche," which for us meant youth and freedom. It was the beginning of a wonderful adventure. Saint Laurent demonstrated that fashion is a dialogue between the designer and women, between the designer and the street.

It is only a step from Chanel to Yves Saint Laurent. Chanel was the first to realize that women were not objects. She liberated them. Saint Laurent, in turn, saw that women had to be empowered. By taking clothes off men's shoulders and putting them onto women's, he gave them that power. But the result was not androgyny. Each to his own! Wearing men's clothes brought out a woman's femininity, her sensuality.

So it was that Yves Saint Laurent ventured into the social arena in 1966. Is it any surprise? He had just turned thirty and had already been steeped in the fashion world for ten years. In an interview he gave Dino Buzzati in *Corriere della Sera* in 1961 before the opening of his fashion house, Saint Laurent said: "What interests me is to make dresses that are really useful, that any woman could wear."

Pierre Bergé

French *Elle* announces the opening of Saint Laurent Rive Gauche, with photographs of several of the store's soon-to-be-popular designs, such as the black velvet dress and the tuxedo.
French *Elle*, September 29, 1966.
Photographs by Yoshida.

EVENEMENT:
LA HAUTE COUTURE DEBARQUE RIVE GAUCHE

SAINT-LAURENT OUVRE BOUTIQUE A SAINT-GERMAIN Formidable ! Saint-Laurent devient « abordab
vient d'ouvrir une boutique rive gauche. Et on
trouver par exemple ça : 1. Une robe de trico
brun, orange et rouge, empiècement et ourlet
(270 F). On la ceinture d'anneaux dorés (45 F).
des pendentifs en émail (85 F). 2. Ce manteau
nage marine à boutons dorés, une martingale

e dos (480 F). Bas rouges (cachemire). Chaussu-
ernies à boucles (Roger Vivier pour Saint-Lau-
3. Merveilleuse jupe en daim moutarde la taille
he basse, à découpe arrondie surpiquée. Pas
et. On « coupe »... (Mini : 200 F. Normale : 250 F).
lleur à chevrons gris et blanc. La veste : un
long à martingale. Jupe à grosse ceinture

(700 F). Bas résille (20 F). 5. Smoking noir. En grain
de poudre avec revers et « baguettes » de satin
Haute ceinture drapée (750 F). Blouse blanche volan-
tée (150 F). 6. Une des fameuses robes de petite fille
modèle de Saint-Laurent. Velours noir. Organza tuyau-
té. Taille haute soulignée d'un ruban de faille, noué
en nœud plat dans le dos (480 F). Bas brillants (40 F).

DOWN WITH THE RITZ . . . LONG LIVE THE STREET!

YVES SAINT LAURENT, AUGUST 1965

The Voyage to Rive Gauche

Jéromine Savignon

"Down with the Ritz…long live the street!"[1] This heartfelt exclamation by Yves Saint Laurent during an interview in the summer of 1965 was meant in part to amuse and provoke, but it was also the apt expression of an intuitive and deliberate train of thought that was leading him gradually and inevitably toward the rue de Tournon on Paris's Left Bank and the creation of Saint Laurent Rive Gauche.

The time was ripe for it. There was a general sense of excitement and expectation, a longing for something new, all of which was clearly registered by Saint Laurent—the "Little Prince of Couture," the "Beatle of the rue Spontini"[2]—who was always fascinated by the present moment. He sensed the social upheavals just around the corner, envisioning the world to come, in which he intended to be "the couturier who [thinks] about today's women."[3] "Between the voyage to Cythera on the one hand and the voyage to the moon on the other, there is room for an era, our own, which no one seems to be paying attention to," said Saint Laurent. Often torn between Proust and Andy Warhol, he was preparing, according to Françoise Giroud, editor of the newsweekly *L'Express*, to "capture" one of the most powerful currents of the 1960s: "the imperialism of the young."[4]

Just twenty-one when he created his first, hugely successful collection for Dior, the "trapeze" line, and only a few years older when he presided over his own worldly temple on the rue Spontini, Yves

1. Patrick Thévenon, "Le couturier qui a pensé aux femmes d'aujourd'hui," *Candide,* August 15, 1965.

2. Ibid.

3. Ibid.

4. Françoise Giroud, "Juliette et Messaline," *L'Express,* August 4–10, 1969.

I AM CONVINCED WE
ARE ON THE BRINK
OF AN UPHEAVAL IN
OUR ART OF LIVING
COMPARABLE TO THE
SEA CHANGE FOLLOWING
THE INTERNATIONAL
ART DECO EXPOSITION.

YVES SAINT LAURENT, AUGUST 1965

Yves Saint Laurent, Paris, 1968.
Photograph by Marie Cosindas.

Saint Laurent had learned, by devoting himself wholly to couture and working from sketch to sketch, that fashion is above all "a change in attitudes."[5] More than a pencil line, a dress is a gesture. It is made not to be looked at but to be invested with attitudes, those of a woman-as-drawing, projected into a dream of seduction that willfully ignores maxims of elegance. "A way of living rather than a way of dressing."[6]

In fact, the times were rapidly changing, and the affectations of haute couture, an increasingly vacillating and reclusive domain, were becoming apparent. "What is outmoded…is the whole system, the presentations, the private clients, the ordering."[7] The city was seeing the arrival of a new generation of "Amazonian" women,[8] who were feverishly awaiting "the suggestion of *something else*; a fashion that would fragmentarily suggest another world and a few instruments for getting there."[9] This was what passionately interested Yves Saint Laurent at the time: women's directness in dealing with their lives, their way of being, of wanting to exist, to express themselves, and to have fun, all of which made him yearn "to not just be a great couturier anymore."[10]

There had been, among the great fashion houses, a few embryonic attempts at starting boutiques that sold trinkets and simplified copies of couture creations. In 1964, Saint Laurent himself had pushed the whole idea to a new level with his "boutique" collection of thirty-five designs, including a panoply of accessories, to dress any woman—not just royal princesses or Zizi Jeanmaire—twenty-four hours a day according to the impulse of the moment. It was a "little collection," easy and contemporary, allowing a woman to live in "Saint Laurent from morning to night," and yet it maintained the standards of the "big collection." The designs were "masterworks of charm," using the full range of Saint Laurent's vocabulary, but lightened, simplified, and presented in a stripped-down environment intended to derail the ritual ceremony of gilded Napoleon III chairs. The collection was exhibited in a space that showcased the clean lines of Scandinavian design and the International Style—brown

5. Claude Berthod, televised interview with Yves Saint Laurent, *Dim Dam Dom*, March 10, 1968.

6. Ibid.

7. Ibid.

8. An expression first coined by Helmut Newton.

9. Jean-Jacques Schuhl, *Rose Poussière* (Paris: Gallimard, 1972) p. 46.

10. Claude Berthod, televised interview with Yves Saint Laurent, *Dim Dam Dom*, March 10, 1968.

satin, black leather, flocked silk in beige and dark brown, mannequins with wooden heads carved by François-Xavier and Claude Lalanne. At the time, French *Vogue* enthusiastically endorsed the new "boutique" spirit: "If you like finding a waterproof suit for your weekends and a long dress for your evenings all in one place, if you like to enter a changing room in your underwear and come out with a full wardrobe, then yes, you have the 'boutique' spirit.... The Boutique Yves Saint Laurent is for you."[11]

The revolution signed "YSL" was under way and nothing could stop it. With his haute couture collection in homage to Mondrian a great success and U.S. journalists calling him the "King of Paris" and "Saint Laurent the Young, Yves the Magnificent,"[12] he joyously proclaimed in an interview published on October 11, 1965, in *Women's Wear Daily*: "I would love to see my Mondrian dresses all over Saint-Germain-des-Prés."

"But there wasn't just art, there was also the street. [Already] Yves Saint Laurent was looking at the bodies that would ascend the barricades in 1968, and he wanted to dress them. He took stock of the beatnik and Pop Art movements, and what he did was not so much to retrieve them as to ennoble them by giving them recognition."[13]

For these young, curious, active women, who were not "blasé billionaires"[14] but career-oriented achievers with neither the inclination nor the means to dress in haute couture, the young designer imagined the concept and the cultural idiosyncrasy of Saint Laurent Rive Gauche—his ready-to-wear, "his absolute idea,"[15] his manifesto as an enfant terrible, his conviction.

Yves Saint Laurent was "the first to truly formulate and incorporate into practice"[16] the ideological revolution of ready-to-wear that was radically independent from the closed circle of couture and that had its own global creative identity and prices that were deliberately accessible. "I think that the future is in ready-to-wear, because it's something new and full of hope. There is enormous unfairness in the prices of haute couture.... What I'd really like is to be Prisunic [a popular department store], to make much less expensive dresses...so that everyone could come in and buy them."[17]

11. French *Vogue*, October 1964.

12. *Jardin des Modes*, Panorama of haute couture, fall–winter 1965–1966.

13. Hervé Guibert, "Aux couleurs des saisons, les toiles peintes d'un voyant charmeur," *Le Monde*, December 8, 1983.

14. *Le Journal du Dimanche*, August 15, 1965.

15. Interview with Pierre Bergé, October 8, 2009.

16. Françoise Sagan, "Saint Laurent par Françoise Sagan," French *Elle*, March 3, 1980.

17. Claude Berthod, televised interview with Yves Saint Laurent, *Dim Dam Dom*, March 10, 1968.

Speaking recently, Pierre Bergé said: "I'm not sure that Saint Laurent himself realized the extent to which he was driving the discussion, but that discussion was very social in nature. We very much admired Terence Conran's idea for Habitat."[18] Terence Conran, of course, was the man who "just wanted everyone in the world to have a well-designed salad bowl."[19] "For us," Pierre Bergé went on, "that was what creating in the present meant, and we even thought about buying Les Trois Quartiers department store to bring our dream to fruition."[20] With great excitement, Yves Saint Laurent and Pierre Bergé then embarked on their Rive Gauche venture, a collaborative effort that quickly became a point of entry into the style of Yves Saint Laurent for thousands of women around the world.

The designer, who lived at the time on place Vauban in the seventh arrondissement, was firmly ensconced in the Left Bank. He liked the neighborhood, its cafés, its antique stores, its bohemian air of fantasy and freedom. This was, perhaps, a reaction to his overly straitlaced childhood. A child prodigy, he had been catapulted into adulthood by his early successes and cloistered in the world of haute couture without ever being allowed to enjoy his childhood or act out his beatnik dreams or do anything irresponsible. His original idea was to open a shop that would cater to students in the Latin Quarter, Saint-Germain-des-Prés, and to any young woman who dared to opt for seduction over elegance. It would operate as a sort of drugstore for fashion—open every day until midnight! Among the hole-in-the-wall frame shops and bookstores along the run-down rue de Tournon, which climbs peacefully toward the Luxembourg Gardens and the Senate, there was an old antique store, long and narrow like a hobbit hole, that had once been a bakery. It would become the first Saint Laurent Rive Gauche store.

Its transformation, conceived by Yves Saint Laurent, was put in the hands of the young Isabelle Hebey. A lover of glass and gleaming metal, she was one of the first to use steel in interior decoration. The store

18. Interview with Pierre Bergé, October 8, 2009.

19. Antonia Williams, "Habitat Man," British *Vogue*, February 1974.

20. Interview with Pierre Bergé, October 8, 2009.

Catherine Deneuve and Yves Saint Laurent, with a sculpture by Niki de Saint-Phalle behind them, at the opening of the first Saint Laurent Rive Gauche store, 21 rue de Tournon, Paris, September 26, 1966. Photograph by Alain Nogues.

American *Vogue*,
December 1966.
Photographs by
Jean-Jacques Bugat.

VOGUE'S OWN
BOUTIQUE

OF SUGGESTIONS, FINDS, AND OBSERVATIONS

Paris: Saint Laurent turns left, crosses the river and, everybody—watch out!

Let Yves Saint Laurent loose on the Left Bank and what happens is just the best. When a designer like Yves—with his eye for wit, elegance, his sense for what's what today, for proportion, the perfect touch—decides to get into the boutique business, you know it's not going to be any piddly little bit of business. There it is—on the Rive Gauche at 21 rue de Tournon (right)—the first of many Saint Laurent boutiques to come—a smashing, bold, handsome boîte of a boutique—crash, gnash with colour—Chinese lacquer red, orange, purple, icy blue, lime, glass, chrome. . . . And clothes, clothes, clothes, superb ones—1967 modern in the very best sense, made of the best fabrics, with the best workmanship, and better than best prices. . . . It's really like haute couture now being filtered through the métier of the boutique. Yves's venture *could* change the face of things for a lot of superb designers everywhere. . . . And everybody is there. Françoise Hardy's there (left), popping in front of the bigger than life portrait of old Yves himself that hangs on a door. . . .

Left: Françoise Hardy—the visage Oh-so-stern, but the look so adorable—in Saint Laurent's long black velvet smock tippetted with a flute of a white organdie collar. About $90. . . .

Right: Françoise Hardy larking along the rue de Tournon in one of Saint Laurent's superb wool knits—simple but subtly cut tubes pointed up with colour—just right. Françoise's—navy with licks of yellow at the neck, cuffs. $37. . . .

Left: Françoise Hardy in three of the besties in Saint Laurent's Rive Gauche boutique. Far left: The incomparable black "smoking," just like the one in Yves's haute couture collection. $100. Centre, left: The great raincoat, slick yellow vinyl down the middle, thick woolly knit in the sleeves. About $76. Tapestry boots to order, $80. Near left: Yellow and Confederate-blue wool Tattersall pants tailleur, $95. . . .

BUGAT

was inaugurated on September 26, 1966, with an all-day open house. Standing in as the store's godmother was Catherine Deneuve, looking very *Belle de Jour*[21] and at the same time very Saint Laurent in her dress with blue and white chevrons and her little navy coat with its high half belt and gold buttons. There was an air of excitement, of lightheartedness, of joyful improvisation. Everyone was ecstatic. With the smile of a delighted child, the slightly shy couturier, looking like a pop-culture dandy in his green velvet Renoma sheath jacket, greeted his guests personally as they entered his "time capsule," which had been liberally spritzed with his Y eau de toilette.

Everything about the setting, with its startling contrasts, testified to Yves Saint Laurent's keen anticipation of the moment. Oxblood red carpets and Japanese-style open-worked metal screens; exposed stone and lacquered beams; long, massive aluminum rectangles for the clothing racks and display cases; lots of glass; huge round mirrors; deep purple banquettes, their foam cushions sheathed in nylon jersey by Olivier Mourgue, the poet of wise ideas and crazy dreams that were featured in *2001: A Space Odyssey*; the filtered light of Isamu Noguchi's "lamps"; and, suspended from the wall, the sharp neorealist touch of Raymond Hains's giant matchbooks. And directly across from the entrance, at the back, was the enormous portrait of Yves Saint Laurent by Eduardo Arroyo. In the small garden court were several "Nanas" by Niki de Saint-Phalle, rescued from the decor of Roland Petit's ballet *In Praise of Folly,* standing witness to the artistic curiosity and open-mindedness of the store's presiding spirits. Art was to be a signature of Saint Laurent Rive Gauche, and two large Jean Dunand vases were soon selected as the sole decoration for the window of a second Paris store at 38 rue du Faubourg Saint-Honoré.

The first store's staggering success brought an invasion of parked and double-parked cars to the quiet rue de Tournon. "Nothing like it had

21. Filming for Luis Buñuel's *Belle de Jour*, starring Catherine Deneuve, would begin on October 10, 1966.

ever been seen!" says Clara Saint, who was then Rive Gauche's young press attaché.[22] Catherine Deneuve also has a vivid memory of it: "It was so surprising, so unexpected, to find within reach on hangers all the things that represented Right Bank luxury and haute couture quality, but reinterpreted as ready-to-wear. And we didn't begin to suspect the incredible consequences that the success of this project would have."[23]

Drawn initially by curiosity, fashion editors were wowed by the reasonable prices and floored by the perfection of the designs. They vied for the privilege of holding impromptu shoots, either in the street or in front of the portrait of the couturier with his arms crossed. American *Vogue* trumpeted: "Paris: Saint Laurent turns left, crosses the river, and everybody—watch out!" Also: "Paris: Regardez! The new Yves Saint Laurent's."

This "little spontaneous unit,"[24] which invented the transgressive notion of a Saint Laurent design outside of haute couture, became a not-to-be-missed attraction. People elbowed their way in and stood in line into the wee hours to buy a Rive Gauche outfit. Simple little things, deliciously tailored, sized from F34 to F42 (American sizes 2 to 10), easy to wear, easy to sell. They could be carried away right then and there, wrapped in tissue paper in a shopping bag emblazoned with the orange and pink squares of the boutique's logo—a logo especially designed for Rive Gauche by Yves Saint Laurent himself and the perfume designer Pierre Dinand. It was rare for anyone to leave with only one item: a skirt at rue de Tournon was almost always coordinated with one of the matching tops or knitted-wool sweaters; and the salesgirls were trained to suggest looks, pairings, and accessories so that a woman could, according to her mood, invent a basic outfit for herself with many different combinations, all of them youthful and made for the joy of pleasing, of seducing—*Just suppose I meet him*. More than a wardrobe, these clothes represented a style at unbeatable prices. "A Happening" was the headline in *Elle*: "Haute couture crosses to the Left Bank. Saint Laurent becomes 'affordable.' "[25]

22. Interview with Clara Saint, October 26, 2009.

23. Interview with Catherine Deneuve, November 5, 2009.

24. Interview with Dominique Deroche, former director of communications at Yves Saint Laurent.

25. "Évènement: la haute couture débarque Rive Gauche," French *Elle*, September 29, 1966.

"WITH HIS 'RIVE GAUCHE YVES SAINT LAURENT THE WAY FOR A REVOLU AS THE REVOLUTION BR CHRISTIAN DIOR IN 194

LE MONDE, JULY 23, 1969

READY-TO-WEAR,
SEEMS TO BE PAVING
TION AS IMPORTANT
OUGHT ABOUT BY
WITH HIS NEW LOOK."

At the rue de Tournon store, you might find, for example, "a wool knit dress in brown, orange, and red stripes (270 francs), belted with a chain of gold rings (45 francs). Add an enamel pendant (85 francs),"[26] before slipping on the famous little uniform coat of navy wool with gold buttons (480 francs). Fishnet stockings (20 francs) and black patent-leather boots (230 francs) complete the outfit. Then of course, there were the famous dresses in black velvet and white guipure (350 and 600 francs).

And who could resist the tuxedo in black grain de poudre, with satin lapels, outseam stripes, and a broad belt (750 francs), along with its indispensable ruffled white blouse (150 francs)? Catherine Deneuve loved it and wore it when she posed next to her Pygmalion of a couturier. "I created this store because I wanted to see my dresses being worn in the streets.... A girl can buy herself an outfit here for 250 francs,"[27] Saint Laurent crowed to all the journalists at his store's opening.[28] "We sold to people who fell in love with the clothes," said Dominique Deroche.

For Yves Saint Laurent, the Rive Gauche line offered a place of freedom, one that was never hemmed in by the constraints of haute couture, the tyrannies of the line, and the rigid ukases of ritual or meticulous dress codes. At times, in the middle of a season, he might suddenly decide: "'I have an idea! Let's make three dresses.' He would make them and it would amuse him enormously."[29]

Preparations for the extensive Rive Gauche runway shows of the succeeding years—the archetype will always be the 283 separate runs of the "Carmen" collection of spring–summer 1977—would unfold with the same spontaneous contemporaneity. Choices were made by instinct, the way you might browse through your dressing room and follow the "elective affinities" of chance and the dizzying prospect of infinite combinations.

And when the inclination to dress differently came over him and he wanted "to do something so that things change,"[30] Yves Saint Laurent

26. "Évènement: la haute couture débarque Rive Gauche," French *Elle*, September 29, 1966.

27. In 1966, 5 francs equaled approximately 1 U.S. dollar. So, for example, 250 francs is equal to approximately 50 U.S. dollars. In comparison with the prices quoted above, the haute couture dress featured on page 55 was priced at 5,500 francs, or approximately 1,100 dollars.

28. Quoted by Carmen Tessier, *France Soir*, September 27, 1966.

29. Interview with Clara Saint, October 26, 2009.

30. Claude Berthod, "Les hommes nouveaux que nous prépare Saint Laurent," French *Elle*, May 5, 1969.

Sketch by Yves Saint Laurent
of a vinyl coat with knitted-
wool sleeves.
Saint Laurent Rive Gauche,
autumn–winter 1966.

LA BOUTIQUE

THE ACADEMICIANS, FILLED WITH NEW YOUTHFULNESS, HAVE MOUNTED THE COUNTERATTACK ON THE FAUVES.

St. Laurent Rive Gauche blazed the way and its explosive success convinced everybody that the couture of the near future is tied unquestionably to ready-to-wear offsprings.

MORE BIG GUNS ARE BEING BROUGHT UP.

Dior is getting ready a boutique about as large as Rive Gauche, in the Dior building. The Miss Dior collection which Philippe Guibourge is designing for the boutique will be available in Dior outlets elsewhere in Europe.

If Cardin can get his bustling affairs in order, two of his boutiques will open on the Left Bank.

Even Ungaro who adores carefully tailoring his things for the private clients, is negotiating with a rtw manufacturer.

PIERRE BERGE KEEPS SMILING AN I-TOLD-YOU-SO SMILE as he hops about between the Rue Spontini and the cash register at the Rue de Tournon (Rive Gauche).

Last month St. Laurent Rive Gauche brought the house more cash than Spontini. The boutique is cash-and-carry and they've been carrying like crazy. "We've turned over $100,000 in October," says M. Berge. "About a third of that was gross profit."

Rive Gauche probably could have sold much more in October,

but the instant success caught Mendes, the major manufacturer, off guard, and loads of things were sold out.

NOW THE FAST-MOVING STOCK HAS BEEN FILLED IN.

Jerry Silverman visited the Rue de Tournon, was amazed by the plenty. "It's a bright, tremendous collection cut in depth. There's probably no other store in Paris moving merchandise in such an American way: A girl can go in and get her color and size and walk out with her purchase . . . and it's very well coordinated. It's a wonderful wardrobe look for any young girl."

Mr. Silverman found the clothing "very well made" but thinks they could be manufactured more cheaply (dress prices are from $ to $130) in the United States because of the volume American manufacturers do. Mendes, however, plans to lower prices as volume increases and M. Berge confirms that a price cut of about 20 per cent is in the works for next season.

THE PILOT RUE DE TOURNON BOUTIQUE is wholly owned by St. Laurent, but the house doesn't want to take part in any of the other boutiques which will begin opening in Europe beginning next year.

The formula will remain the same as for the Marseille boutique already opened. Brilliantly simple: YSL will do nothing but choose the licensed boutique owners, design models and collect about 10 per cent net profit on the wholesalers' receipt. No investment, no administrative headaches, no burden on the retailer.

FAIT "BOOM"

11-21-666

The plans for the long run are for Yves himself to become a sort of captain of a team of ready-to-wear designers. He'll give ideas to be developed, or approve ideas coming from the rest of the team.

For the moment the ready-to-wear designing has been tiring work, weighing on his shoulders alone. He's trying to find someone who could at least do a lot of the legwork between himself and the manufacturers and fabric people.

YVES HAS ALREADY DESIGNED THE BASIC PART OF THE SPRING COLLECTION, but the idea, as M. Berge points out, is to a "constant ragout of things going all year 'round.'"

Since the late September opening in the Rue de Tournon, many new items have been put in circulation. One of them, a black velvet coat (sketched left) has become a bestseller.

The boutique is not just a ready-to-wear subsidiary of the couture house. It's a way of "amortizing" couture ideas.

The pop models Yves' private clients shied away from are selling well in boutique adaptations. Alexandre has turned that red-lipped black dress into a uniform for the girls in his hairdressing salon.

The ideas are amortized over a long period of time. M. Berge expects the constantly bubbling boutique collection to be more resistant to datedness than if it was a strict two-season affair. And old couture models, with a few changes, prolong their life in the boutique. Another best seller is the knitted-sleeve vinyl raincoat born in a couture collection of a few seasons ago (sketched second from left.)

THE BOUTIQUES OUT OF TOWN BRING PARIS (FOR WHICH THE PROVINCIALS HUNGER) RIGHT TO THE PROVINCES.

Marseille, which has half the six salespeople that the Rue de Tournon has, is earning about $1,300 a day, M. Berge says.

The salespeople are young and good-looking. "The rapport between the salespeople and the customers is marvelous," says Mr. Silverman.

The salesgirls, who wear the boutique clothes, are at the same time kind of mannequins and enviable sisters to the customers. The two young boys in the Rue de Tournon seem to be having success with the flirtatious dames d'un certain age who come to the Rue de Tournon in large numbers as if to the Fountain of Youth.

M. Berge expects the number of St. Laurent Rive Gauche boutiques to number about 20 in France in the next few years. He isn't limiting the number, doesn't believe there's a risk of saturation.

For the United States, there's no decision yet. Maybe in two years a boutique will open there. Maybe the idea will be limited to Europe. Next year, Toulouse will open, and in 1968 Bordeaux, Lyon and Nantes.

"We're in no hurry," smiles M. Berge. "Our policy is 'Wait and See'."

BUT WHILE ALL THE OTHER COUTURIERS UNTIL NOW HAVE BEEN **WAITING,** ST. LAURENT HAS BEEN **SEEING** AN EYEFUL OF PROFITS.

—G. Y. DRYANSKY, Paris Bureau

had only to go a few steps to 17 rue de Tournon to establish his first boutique for men. The whole Saint Laurent wardrobe, starting with the safari jacket, was offered there. "Everything, except suits!"[31] Saint Laurent said: "I design for free men, and what I offer them is not a new 'line,' which would only be another constraint, but the freedom to wear all year round, whatever the season, the same middy blouse, with or without a sweater, with a matched or an unmatched pant.... To have only clothes that are weightless: supple pants, unlined jackets, comfortable shirts."[32] All the boys and all the girls of a particular age, excited by a sense of fashion that was new and untried, fell hard for Saint Laurent Rive Gauche. "Today, they are more than equals: very close without being the same.... They live the same lives, so it's normal that they should wear the same jeans, the same shetlands, the same middy blouses, the same tunics."[33]

Yves Saint Laurent and Pierre Bergé were at Rive Gauche almost every day. Sales were brisk. In the store, "it was a madhouse from morning till night."[34] The flying elbows and general congestion reached such proportions that sometimes even Pierre Bergé manned a cash register, and a young woman soon had to be hired whose sole duty was to tirelessly fold and put away all the clothes that the eager shoppers had scattered to the four winds in their frenzied enthusiasm. Even the clients who normally bought haute couture crossed the Seine to have a look. Seduced, they arranged to have selections from the Rive Gauche line sent to them at rue Spontini. For women of the Right Bank, 21 rue de Tournon was at the absolute center of all that was newest at Saint Laurent. When they crossed the Seine, they felt the excitement of letting go of the shibboleths of their too-sixteenth-arrondissement elegance on their first voyage into the very heart of the Saint Laurent spirit. It was there, in the Saint-Germain neighborhood and nowhere else, that they found the cream of the collection and became even more Saint Laurent, even more Parisian.

Elle magazine suggested that its readers visit—as did celebrities Mireille Darc and Catherine Deneuve—during the relatively quiet lunch

31. Interview with Clara Saint, October 26, 2009.

32. Claude Berthod, "Les hommes nouveaux que nous prépare Saint Laurent," French *Elle*, May 5, 1969.

33. Ibid.

34. Claude Berthod, "Le prêt-à-porter sort ses 'griffes,'" French *Elle*, October 26, 1967.

Page 33: A wool
jersey dress (detail).
Saint Laurent
Rive Gauche,
autumn–winter 1966.
Photograph by
Sophie Carre.

Left: The first tuxedo
by Saint Laurent
Rive Gauche, worn by
Françoise Hardy,
autumn–winter 1966.

hour. Women competed for the ring belts whose clinking gold metal made background music for the wearer. Another memorable addiction was the white silk scarf with the YSL monogram, which the couturier pulled prematurely from circulation after the entire audience at a premiere at the Olympia Theater featuring Zizi Jeanmaire seemed to be waving the Saint Laurent banner. On the other hand, *Elle* warned: "You'll never find on Thursday the dress you scouted out on Tuesday, and you'll often have to wait two weeks for the shelves to be restocked."[35]

Early on, Yves Saint Laurent realized that women not only wanted but also needed a certain stability in their wardrobe so that, as free entities, they could find and assert themselves, grow in confidence, and be happy. His genius was to have sensed the right moment for investing young, ordinary, timeless clothes with the Saint Laurent spirit, thus providing the foundation for the modern woman's wardrobe. The refrain would be Rive Gauche, punctuated by all of the top Rive Gauche hits.

Like others of the couturier's basic designs, the tuxedo—reflecting troubled, and troubling, urges—traveled from rue Spontini to Rive Gauche, becoming "the absolute emblem of Yves Saint Laurent" along the way.[36] Created for the 1966–1967 autumn–winter collection and hailed by the international fashion press, the tuxedo won only a *succès d'estime* from the couture clients. But when the singer Françoise Hardy entered the rue de Tournon store shortly after its opening and saw the tuxedo, she tried it on and immediately picked it for her next gala. The tuxedo, known as "le smoking," was made for her. Within days, a photo appeared on the front page of *France Soir* and ignited a burst of sales. The legend was born.

The tuxedo offers a good example of the early crossover between Yves Saint Laurent's haute couture and his ready-to-wear. The connection, despite a stated independence, was always strong. And the influence didn't always run in the expected direction. Themes and ideas often migrated from the ready-to-wear line to the haute couture house, rather

35. Claude Berthod,
"Le prêt-à-porter sort
ses 'griffes,'" French *Elle*,
October 26, 1967.

36. Interview with Pierre
Bergé, October 8, 2009.

READY-TO-WEAR IS
I AM CONCERNED
A SORT OF SUB—
IT'S THE FUTURE.
TO CREATE READY-

YVES SAINT LAURENT, FRENCH *ELLE*, OCTOBER 26, 1967

NOT, AS FAR AS
A LESSER GENRE,
HAUTE COUTURE;
IT'S VERY EXCITING
TO-WEAR.

An article revealing
the rapid expansion
of the brand,
with images of
Saint Laurent
Rive Gauche stores
in Paris, Grenoble,
Rome, Bordeaux,
Madrid, Munich,
and Nice.
French *Vogue*,
February 1969.
Photographs
by Publifoto,
P.-L. Thiessard,
Michaël Doster,
Pierre Burdin.

LES BOUTIQUES
DE VOGUE

BRAVO A TOUS LES "SAINT LAURENT-RIVE GAUCHE"!

à Paris...

Marraine de la première "Rive Gauche" inaugurée en 19
21, rue de Tournon, **Catherine Deneuve** en tailleur-pantal

à Paris...

38, Fg-St-Honoré. **Betty Catroux** en combinaison no

à Grenoble...

5, place St-Laurent. **Catherine Serre**, une écharpe fran

à Madrid...

100, Calle Serrano. Devant le portrait d'Yves Saint Laurent, la **marquise de Griñon** en redingote noire à boutons dorés.

à Munich...

Buerkleinstrasse 10. **Madame von Chamier** en tenue lamé.

▼

Les "Saint Laurent-Rive Gauche" font boule de neige. Aujourd'hui dix-neuf dans le monde. Demain, vingt de plus en Amérique. Au printemps, fleuriront Lausanne et Berlin. Adoptez, pour le meilleur prix possible, la plus jolie mode qui soit.

à Bordeaux...

29, cours Clemenceau. **Madame Christian Laffontan** en robe longue de jersey blanc.

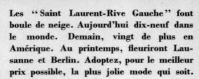

Rome...

, via Borgognona. La principessa **arizzina Odescalchi**, ses achats termi-. Les boutiques se ressemblent tou-; décor : Isabelle Hebey. Vitrines dées métal, tapis rouge orangé, siè- violets d'Olivier Mourgue, lampions.

▶

à Nice...

7, rue Paradis. Sac en bandoulière et long pendentif doré, **Madame Jean-Pierre Vic**, jolie sœur d'Yves Saint Laurent.

▲

LES BOUTIQUES
DE VOGUE *(Suite)*

à Toulouse...
1, place Wilson. Pardessus à chevrons pour **Madame Pierre Jonquères d'Oriola.**

à Genève... ▲
51, rue du Rhône. **Marina Doria**
devant le choix des ceintures...

à Saint-Tropez...▲
41, rue Gambetta. **La comtesse Charles
de Rohan Chabot** avec l'écharpe à succès.

à Paris... ▲
46, av. Victor-Hugo. Les pantalons larges **d'Albina du Boisrouvray.**

à Bruxelles...

2, boulevard de Waterloo. La robe-kilt à carreaux sur la **princesse Antoinette de Mérode.**

à Zurich...

trehlgasse 26. La **princesse Theresa Fürsenberg** dans le ciré dont tout Paris raffole.

à New York...

855, Madison Avenue. Un autre imperméable court, porté par **Madame Hilarios Theodoracopulos.**

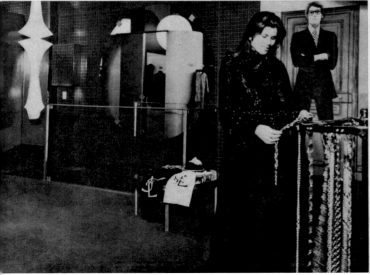

à Lyon... 10, rue des Archers (ci-dessus).
à Hambourg... Jungfernstieg 48.
à Venise... Hôtel Cipriani.

◀ à Milan...

18, via Santo Spirito. Tunique-pantalon scintillant et ceintures-chaînes pour la **comtesse Dona Dalle Rose.**

than vice versa—a perfect example is the memorable "Ballets Russes" collection. Such are the vagaries of the heart...

It was a tidal wave. "Bravo to all the new 'Saint Laurent Rive Gauches'!" ran a French *Vogue* headline in February 1969. "Today there are 19 around the world. Tomorrow there will be another 20 in the U.S. This spring, two more will flower in Lausanne and Berlin. Choose, at the best price imaginable, the loveliest fashions anywhere." All the big European cities were reveling in Saint Laurent: Lyon, Marseille, Grenoble, Nice, Bordeaux, Rome, Madrid, Munich, Toulouse, Geneva, Saint-Tropez, Brussels, Zurich, London, Hamburg, Venice, and Milan.

In New York, the store was an extraordinary success. Pierre Bergé still remembers the telephone call he received the night that Rive Gauche opened at 855 Madison Avenue in September 1968. The police had to contain the hysterical crowd that was trying to storm the aluminum tunnel of the new temple to Rive Gauche. It was insanity! American women, with Faye Dunaway and Lauren Bacall leading the charge, wanted to own the vinyl raincoat, the kilt dress, the monogrammed scarf, and the little tube dress of multicolored jersey that Paris had gone crazy for. They all saw themselves already in the black satin jumpsuit worn deeply unzipped by Betty Catroux, Yves's confidante and his accomplice in their shared fantasies of "sadistic or precocious children."[37] Betty, whom Yves referred to as his twin sister and female incarnation—posing regally, nonchalantly, and totally YSL—was a kind of messiah for "the fall of a stereotype, the end of a convention, the expression of the rhythm and movement of our time."[38] American women came to buy a handsome piece of clothing rather than a label or an image, "a basic wardrobe item they could count on,"[39] perfect for their lives, for life. This was the very essence of the Rive Gauche spirit.

In the midst of this euphoria came a great flop, the scandal of the infamous haute couture collection of summer 1971, Retro 40. This stinging failure gave Yves Saint Laurent the opportunity to think deeply about the

37. "La vilaine Lulu," French *Vogue*, August 1964.

38. Philippe Labro, "Yves Saint Laurent: 'La mode d'aujourd'hui c'est démodé,'" *Le Journal du Dimanche*, February 2, 1969.

39. Claude Berthod, "La haute couture: sept ans pour mourir ou six mois pour changer?" *Gap*, September 1974.

Betty Catroux,
Yves Saint Laurent, and
Loulou de la Falaise
at the opening of the
first Saint Laurent
Rive Gauche store in
London, New Bond
Street, September 10,
1969.

future of haute couture, sublime but sterile, marginalized, and creating "only nostalgia and prohibitions"[40] because it was no longer connected to life and modern times. This reinforced Saint Laurent's commitment to prêt-à-porter, his passion for it. In the domain of ready-to-wear, he could follow his intuitions about fashion fully and without restraint.

His snip of the shears was radical and "in line with everything he had decided by starting the Rive Gauche line."[41] Yves Saint Laurent's next haute couture collection, pared down to forty designs—and conceived uniquely for his privileged clients—would be presented more quietly. French *Elle* characterized this official decision as "the fashion event of the fall season" and illustrated it with a startling photograph of the designer between two models wearing identical shirtdresses, one as perfect as the other (see pages 54–55). "The one on the left, in ready-to-wear: 650 francs. The one on the right, in haute couture: 5,500 francs."[42] "What I hate more than anything? Snobbishness about money," said Saint Laurent, the "Little Prince of Couture," in a March 1968 television interview. This "shy young man with the soft eyes of a Florentine angel"[43] had already fled to the street, a street that would never stop parading before him.

In another televised interview on October 30, 1971, Yves Saint Laurent delivered his credo with as much calm and conviction as modesty: "I have chosen to present my fashion through my ready-to-wear rather than through my haute couture....I think ready-to-wear is the expression of fashion today. I believe that is where fashion is, and not in haute couture." Yet he admitted to loving haute couture as he might a mistress, neither wanting nor able to do without it. He kept his fashion house going out of respect for the artisans it employed and those who had built it up. The underlying tensions were all too evident: either make the fashion house he had created a success or abandon it to keep alive his ideal. The choice was not an easy one, though his happiness hung on the outcome.

The shock of the 1971 collection was in some sense the final step for Yves Saint Laurent on his quest for internal purity, his long search for

Charlotte Rampling in a green and brown wool crepe dress from the Saint Laurent Rive Gauche collection of autumn–winter 1970. French *Vogue*, September 1970. Photograph by Jeanloup Sieff.

40. Claude Berthod, "La libération de la femme selon Saint Laurent," French *Elle*, March 1, 1971.

41. Interview with Catherine Deneuve, November 5, 2009.

42. Claude Berthod, "Yves Saint Laurent choisit le prêt-à-porter: cette photo explique sa décision," French *Elle*, June 9, 1971.

43. Patrick Modiano, "Collections 70. Le journal de bord chez les couturiers," French *Vogue*, September 1969.

Saint Laurent-Rive Gauche a trouvé en Charlotte Rampling (après " Les Damnés ", elle a terminé " The Ski Bun ") son type de fille, bottée-lacée, blonde, racée, pour son style tout en douceur, tentant, accessible (de 200 à 600 F). (Ci-dessus), robe en crêpe de laine imprimé Liberty vert, brique, marron. (A droite), kilt à la cheville en étamine de laine et chemise en crêpe aux impressions reliure. Gilet de velours. Bottes lacées. Coiffures Carita.

PRÊT - A - PORTER DES COUTURIERS 1971

UNE FILLE SAINT LAURENT

CHARLOTTE RAMPLING
LE JOUR COMME LE SOIR
DANS LA LIBERTÉ DU LIBERTY

Charlotte Rampling in a marbled crepe shirt and wool muslin skirt, velvet vest, and lace-up boots from the Saint Laurent Rive Gauche collection of autumn–winter 1970. French *Vogue*, September 1970.
Photograph by Jeanloup Sieff.

himself through fashion design. He had undergone a sort of psychoanalysis through the tuxedo, the color black, black and its shadows, black and its mysterious glimmerings, and the whole invention of the Saint Laurent woman and her wardrobe. "The big change came when I discovered my own style.... It happened with the tuxedo and the transparent blouse. I became conscious at that time of the body and started a dialogue with women, started to understand better what a modern woman was."[44] The Saint Laurent woman, the Rive Gauche girl! "Secondhand beauty. Made of borrowings. From the songs, the words, the dances of a season. From the necessities of the moment. Due to accidents."[45]

The Rive Gauche girls took many forms: Catherine Deneuve, "the woman he was waiting for, who embodied his style,"[46] the frail, romantic adventuress of *Mississippi Mermaid* who wandered off into the snow, swathed in the velvet and ostrich plumes of her "beautiful coat"[47] from Rive Gauche; Charlotte Rampling, a dreamy Emma Bovary, in lace-up boots and a soft Liberty dress; Talitha Getty, a stormy Amazon princess; Betty Catroux and Loulou de la Falaise, regal, floating; a high-heeled lady of the night with a silk blouse and bare breasts, photographed by Helmut Newton; the model Danielle Varenne, an early inspiration for the Rive Gauche attitude, about whom Saint Laurent said: "She was the one who rid me of all the old-fashioned references and reminiscences, the dust of haute couture.... All the clothes that I made on her... and that collapsed, I saw that I had to get rid of all that for good! She made me go forward"[48]; and then the others, all the others, those long-limbed young ladies, active and determined, whom one meets unexpectedly as they stride briskly through the streets of Paris toward the life of their choice.

Yves Saint Laurent also developed a Rive Gauche fragrance, meant to evoke the same revolutionary message. In the advertisement on page 51, the violence and seduction of love betrayed but unbeaten are fiercely avowed by the flask that, vengeful and deliberate, shatters the mirror while the ad declares: "Rive Gauche is not a fragrance for retiring

44. Quoted by Lynn Young, "The King of Couture," *Newsweek*, November 18, 1974.

45. Jean-Jacques Schuhl, *Rose Poussière* (Paris: Gallimard, 1972) p. 23.

46. Thelma Sweetinburgh, "Yves' Nowgirl," *Women's Wear Daily*, January 6, 1967.

47. A reference to one of Catherine Deneuve's lines in François Truffaut's *Mississippi Mermaid* (1969): "My coat is beautiful... It's lonely there all by itself, it's sad. I should have kept it with me."

48. Quoted by Philippe Labro, "Yves Saint Laurent: 'La mode d'aujourd'hui c'est démodé,'" *Le Journal du Dimanche*, February 2, 1969.

Right: An article proclaiming Talitha Getty's preference for Saint Laurent Rive Gauche, with a photograph of her wearing an ankle-length black dress printed with beige flowers.
French *Vogue*, May 1970.
Photograph by Jeanloup Sieff.

Opposite: Talitha Getty in a printed silk crepe dress and braided leather belt.
Saint Laurent Rive Gauche, spring–summer 1970.
French *Vogue*, May 1970.
Photograph by Jeanloup Sieff.

Talitha Getty opte pour Saint Laurent-rive gauche

Mrs. Paul Getty Jr. habite Rome, voyage beaucoup, aime la fantaisie, la gaîté, la mode. Elle a choisi les toutes dernières robes à la cheville créées par Yves Saint Laurent. *A gauche*, c'est une robe de crêpe noir à larges manches resserrées dans un poignet ; corsage fendu et lacé jusqu'à la taille et jupe évasée en godets. F 875. Haute ceinture et collier de chien en daim noir. *Ci-contre*, en coton noir imprimé de fleurs beiges, une jupe à la cheville et un caraco lacé devant ; manches gigot, basque froncée et décolleté en pointe. F 570. Bottes de toile et cuir. Yves Saint Laurent à la Bottique. Coiffures Christopher de Vidal Sassoon. Voir les adresses page 27.

women."[49] It was, in fact, for those whom Saint Laurent wanted to dress. His innate honesty made him instinctively repudiate any attempt that did not portray life as it was, the actual moment. This provided the real motivation for starting the Rive Gauche line. It gave Saint Laurent "a true joy, like the coincidence between truth and prose, a rare thing."[50]

"The idea of clothing not only the women of Paris in haute couture but all women, to be able to articulate his fashion and offer it to the greatest number, this truly gave him pleasure," says Catherine Deneuve. "He very much wanted to make that luxury available, and it was a personal thing with him, wholehearted."[51]

Playing the Rive Gauche card was, as Pierre Bergé says, a little "like sawing off the branch that you're sitting on, which is going to fall off by itself in any case."[52] But it was also a powerful seminal act for Saint Laurent, who dared to rest his confidence in the street to the point of dedicating his imagination to it, his "aesthetic ghosts," and who made his Rive Gauche fashion a synthesis of perfection and rightness, an instance of "the marvelous silence of clothing," which seemed the entire privilege of ready-to-wear. He had won his bet! The "Little Prince of Couture" had become the "King of Fashion."

"Yves Saint Laurent's modernity lay in demonstrating that haute couture for ladies who have lost everything but their wealth has gone out of fashion. That is why he changed the look of clothes on the street with such enthusiasm. Can an artist dream of anything better?"[53] Like Andy Warhol, he had understood that "the reasoning, the gesture, the intention were all part of the creative act, were as important as the result."[54]

Echoing Diana Vreeland, Pierre Bergé summed it up thus: "This shy young man, living in a bubble of his own, was the most precise, the most adequate man I have ever known. He followed very closely what was happening in the world, and what life had become—and that was wonderful. That is why he belonged to his time."[55]

49. The fragrance Rive Gauche was launched in France in 1971.

50. Françoise Sagan, *Toxique*, illustrations by Bernard Buffet (Paris: René Julliard, 1964). This observation by Sagan was provoked by rereading Proust.

51. Interview with Catherine Deneuve, November 5, 2009.

52. Interview with Pierre Bergé, October 8, 2009.

53. "Diana Vreeland expose un quart de siècle d'YSL," *Libération*, December 7, 1983.

54. Pierre Bergé, *Les Jours s'en Vont Je Demeure* (Paris: Gallimard, 2003).

55. Interview with Pierre Bergé, October 8, 2009.

Advertisement for Rive Gauche perfume, 1979.

Rive Gauche
n'est pas un parfum pour les femmes effacées.

Parfums
YvesSaintLaurent

mafia

WHAT I'D REALLY LIKE IS TO BE PRISUNIC,* TO MAKE MUCH LESS EXPENSIVE DRESSES.

YVES SAINT LAURENT, *DIM DAM DOM*, MARCH 10, 1968

* Prisunic was a department store chain in France.

Page 53:
A shirtdress in printed wool crepe paired with a sweater in chiné knitted wool (detail), Saint Laurent Rive Gauche, autumn–winter 1971. Photograph by Sophie Carre.

Right and pages 56–57: An interview with Yves Saint Laurent in which he explains his preference for designing ready-to-wear clothing, illustrated by photographs that compare ready-to-wear and haute couture, which look very similar but have dramatically different price tags. French *Elle*, June 9, 1971. Photographs by Henri Elwing.

L'événement-mode de la rentrée

Yves Saint Laurent choisit le prêt à porter : cette photo explique sa décision

Yves Saint Laurent a annoncé officiellement sa décision de se consacrer désormais au prêt à porter. Il a des cheveux assez longs, des chemises assez vives, des passions assez violentes, des timidités assez agressives pour qu'on pense d'abord à un coup de tête. Mais l'enfant prodige de la haute couture (il a succédé à Dior à 21 ans) a aujourd'hui 35 ans. C'est l'âge des bilans. L'âge des divorces. L'âge où l'on refait sa vie. Yves Saint Laurent, lui, a décidé de refaire son avenir.

— Pourquoi ?

— Parce que je suis malheureux et que je ne peux plus continuer comme ça, sans cesse écartelé entre ce que j'ai envie de faire et ce que je dois faire. Quand je lance en haute couture des choses que j'aime — mes premiers smokings, mes robes 1945, etc., je fais, financièrement, des bides retentissants. Quand je présente des modèles « commerciaux » les journalistes bâillent plus ou moins poliment. Je suis fatigué de voir la presse s'ennuyer chez moi.

Et je renonce à imposer à des dames qui n'en veulent pas — la plupart sont d'âge respectable — des vêtements qui les traumatisent. Mon vrai public, ce sont les femmes jeunes, les femmes qui travaillent. Je sais que mes prix sont encore prohibitifs pour beaucoup d'entre elles et le vrai problème me semble là : arriver à vendre 300 F le manteau qui coûte actuellement 700 F. Non pas sortir quelques robes de plus ou de moins à 7.000 F, rue Spontini.

— Alors pourquoi ne fermez-vous pas carrément votre maison de couture ?

— Parce que je ne peux pas moralement jeter 150 personnes sur le pavé. Je garde mes clientes particulières pour mes ouvrières et non pas le contraire. Mais je ne pense pas que la haute couture suscite de nouvelles vocations : ni du côté des ouvrières, ni du côté des clientes. Peut-être cela va-t-il durer encore cinq ou dix ans. Pas plus.

— N'est-ce pas un peu mélancolique d'être un liquidateur ?

— C'est au contraire assez excitant d'appartenir à une génération condamnée à tout remettre en question. Il faut tout reconstruire sur des bases nouvelles.

— Avez-vous envie, aussi, de reconstruire les vêtements et les femmes ?

— En tant que créateur, je n'ai jamais été un promoteur de vêtements « cosmiques » et de robes à trous. Et je ne vois pas l'utilité de changer d'une saison à l'autre des vêtements quand ils sont au point. Pas plus les cabans que les blue-jeans, pas plus les smokings que les trench-coats. C'est si vrai que je finissais par faire les mêmes en prêt à porter et en couture. Plus un vêtement est parfait, plus il est simple. Je n'allais quand même pas rajouter des boutons et des fronces pour faire riche !

— Un caban à 4.000 F n'a donc rien de plus qu'un caban à 400 F ?

— Rien. Seules différences : le tissu et le prix. C'est pourquoi il est parfaitement aberrant d'acheter en haute couture un imperméable, un blazer ou un pantalon, bref, finale-

HENRI ELWING

Il y a 4 850 F de différence entre ces deux robes-chemisiers. Celle de gauche, en prêt à porter :
650 F. Celle de droite, en haute couture : 5 500 F.

9

Yves Saint Laurent choisit le prêt à porter

Deux manteaux jumeaux en drap. En prêt à porter, à gauche : 1 000 F. En haute couture, à droite : 4 500 F.

Cabans en drap et pantalons en jersey. Prêt à porter 500 F et 250 F (à g.). Haute couture : 4 000 F et 3 000 F.

Ungaro : « Je ne change rien »

La décision de Saint Laurent pour qui j'ai beaucoup de respect m'attriste énormément. Je continue de penser que la haute couture est un instrument d'expression privilégié. Pour un créateur, c'est la liberté totale. Une liberté que, moi, j'ai payée chèrement et à laquelle je ne renoncerai pas volontairement. Bien sûr, le prêt à porter c'est l'avenir, mais la haute couture n'est pas encore du passé. Elle reste un phénomène vivant. Renoncer à être couturier parce que le prix des vêtements est démentiel — c'est vrai, il l'est — serait comme de renoncer à la peinture parce que seuls quelques-uns peuvent s'acheter des tableaux. Le monde est rempli de beautés que nous ne posséderons jamais, mais il est important qu'elles existent.

---

ment, tous les vêtements de base. Tous les vêtements à vivre.

— **Pensez-vous qu'il est moins aberrant d'y acheter une robe de mousseline qui coûte plus cher qu'une Volkswagen ?**

— Ça c'est autre chose. C'est immoral, anachronique, tout ce que vous voudrez, mais ces robes-là représentent un travail spécifique, irréalisable en prêt à porter. Les femmes qui les commandent font en quelque sorte, involontairement, œuvre de mécènes. Quand la haute couture mourra, ce sera la fin des derniers grands artisanats.

— **Pourquoi la haute couture n'a-t-elle plus aucune influence sur la rue ?**

— Parce que ses prix la destinent à une catégorie de femmes à qui les autres n'ont aucune envie de ressembler. Même pas leurs propres filles.

— **A travers les robes des Puces et toutes les modes-déguisements, les filles les plus modernes cherchent pourtant une certaine image d'elles-mêmes que ne leur donne pas le prêt à porter. N'est-ce pas un autre genre de nostalgie et d'anachronisme ?**

— Non, parce qu'elles portent tout ça avec humour. Rechercher ces vêtements c'est déjà un jeu. Se déguiser c'est un autre jeu. D'ailleurs tous les déguisements ne racontent pas la même histoire. A travers la folie des vêtements militaires, c'est le besoin de vêtements de base, solides et rationnels, qui s'exprime. Les robes longues, les robes 1945, les semelles compensées, les maquillages de cinéma muet expriment au contraire le besoin d'aventure, d'insolite, d'inutile. C'est l'éternel débat : besoin de fidélité et besoin de liberté, besoin de certitudes et besoin de risques. Chacun de nous est un champ de bataille permanent et la contradiction est partout : jersey et taffetas, bonnet tricoté et turban drapé, pantalon et robe à volants n'en sont que la traduction vestimentaire.

— **Comment pensez-vous que va évoluer la mode ?**

— Vers la coexistence des contradictions. D'une part des vêtements de base, pratiquement asexués, pour la vie active : pulls, pantalons, trench-coats, sahariennes. Plus la robe chemisier pour les femmes. D'autre part des vêtements de séduction pour le soir. Ceux-là éphé-

10

Taffetas, volants, romantisme : 1 000 F
(à gauche en prêt à porter). 8 000 F (à
droite en haute couture).

mères et imprévisibles.

— **Avez-vous l'impression aujour-
d'hui, en misant tout sur le prêt à
porter, de repartir à zéro ?**

— Oui et non. Non parce que j'ai
dix-sept ans de métier et que j'ai
beaucoup réfléchi sur tous ces pro-
blèmes. Oui parce que je crois que
les gens se moquent aujourd'hui
totalement des griffes et des mar-
ques et que j'accepte à l'avance
d'être jugé saison par saison, vêtement par vêtement, comme un débu-
tant. Il y a trois ans j'ai dessiné en
noir mes initiales sur une écharpe
en soie blanche et on en a vendu des
milliers. D'autres font encore cela
sur des sacs, sur des pulls, sur des
tissus. Pour moi, cela fait partie des
choses révolues et je n'aurai plus
ni la vanité ni la naïveté de recom-
mencer un geste de ce genre. C'est

Pierre Cardin :
« Je change de dates non de convictions »

*Je présenterai désormais mes
collections en octobre et en
avril. Aux mêmes dates que le
prêt à porter. Mais ce seront
toujours des collections de haute couture. Pour moi la création
est indissociable de la haute
couture qui reste quelque chose
d'irremplaçable et qui ne doit
mourir à aucun prix. C'est là
que sont les vrais créateurs.
C'est là que les confectionneurs
trouvent des idées à adapter.
C'est là que viennent s'habiller
les femmes qui en ont les
moyens. A force de niveler et
de standardiser, on va fabri-
quer un monde où l'on périra
d'ennui. Il y a assez de cime-
tières pour nous égaliser tous.
La vie c'est le choix, la liberté,
la différence. Il n'y a aucune
raison sous prétexte que le pull
et le blue-jean sont des vêtements rationnels et sous prétexte d'égalité d'éliminer la
haute couture qui crée, elle,
des œuvres d'art uniques. L'art,
la beauté resteront indispensa-
bles sous tous les régimes.*

---

typiquement « couturier ».

— **Est-ce que le fait, désormais, de
toujours créer en tenant compte des
prix de revient et de la fabrication
en série ne va pas vous sembler
contraignant ?**

— Je n'ai pas besoin de tissus à 300 F
le mètre et de travaux d'atelier pour
m'exprimer. J'aime ce qui est sophis-
tiqué. Je déteste ce qui est riche. Si
par hasard j'ai besoin de me défou-
ler dans la plume et la paillette,
j'aurai enfin le temps de faire des

HENRI ELWING

Mais cette mousseline nervurée ne
pourra, elle, jamais « descendre dans
la rue » (8 000 F).

costumes de scène : j'adore le théâtre, le cinéma, les comédies musi-
cales, les revues... Et puis, pour moi,
la pire contrainte, c'était l'obligation
de sortir quatre collections par an.
Maintenant mes souffrances seront
divisées par deux. J'ai toujours en-
fanté dans la douleur. Pas au stade
de l'idée, ni du croquis, mais quand
il s'agit de donner la vie à un mor-
ceau de tissu et qu'on n'a plus que
ses ciseaux et ses épingles et que
tout semble rester plat, bête, mort.
Alors il y a toujours un moment où
l'on a envie de tout déchirer et de
partir pour une île au bout du monde pour vivre nu et oublier définiti-
vement ce que veulent dire les mots
crêpe, velours, ratine et, le pire de
tous : collection.

Claude Berthod

11

An article highlighting the revolutionary aspect of couturiers designing ready-to-wear clothing and featuring Saint Laurent Rive Gauche designs, such as the wool coat with flap pockets on the left and the yellow Saint Laurent scarf showcased prominently on the right. French *Elle*, September 9, 1968. Photographs by David Bailey.

DAVID BAILEY

Evolution Révolution: tous les Couturiers lancent leur Prêt à Porter

Le nouveau tailleur de ville, à gauche : veste longue, amincissante, pantalon droit et large, en jersey de laine noir. Les détails : col rabattu, poches à rabat, foulard blanc. Et un chapeau « clin d'œil » : feutre noir et voilette légère (Saint Laurent Rive Gauche, 750 F). Boots en Corfam style croco (Roger Vivier) ∎ A droite, robe-culotte en jersey de laine. Décolleté fendu. Petites emmanchures et « bras longs ». Accessoires : une écharpe de soie, des boucles d'oreilles en émail et perles (Saint Laurent Rive Gauche, 600 F).

REALISATION PEGGY ROCHE ET CHRISTINE RIEDBERGER

I MAKE MY BEST COLLECTIONS WHEN I AM REALLY LIVING, WHEN I GO OUT AND SEE HOW WOMEN ARE DRESSING, HOW THEY WEAR MY DRESSES . . .

AND NOT ONLY AT SOCIAL FUNCTIONS BUT ALSO AT THE SPORTS CENTER AND THE POP CONCERT.

YVES SAINT LAURENT, AUGUST 1965

Sketch by Yves Saint Laurent of an ensemble that pairs a pea jacket with pants in cotton gabardine, Saint Laurent Rive Gauche, spring–summer 1967.

Sketch by Yves Saint Laurent of a wool jersey dress with a buttoned front panel, Saint Laurent Rive Gauche, autumn–winter 1968.

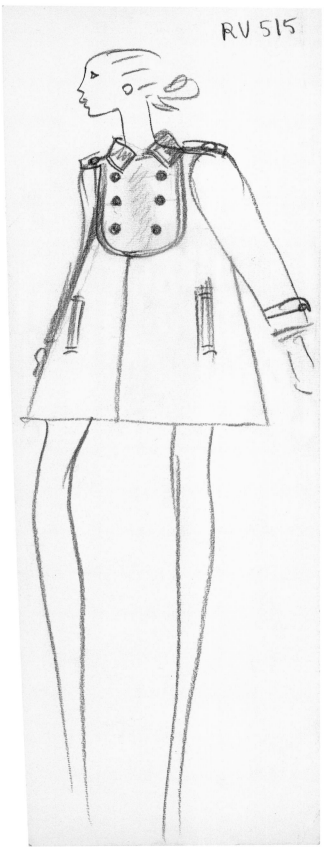

Sketch by Yves Saint Laurent of a terry-cloth dress with an embroidery motif, Saint Laurent Rive Gauche, spring–summer 1967.

Sketch by Yves Saint Laurent of a dress in silk shantung with a necktie in silk twill, Saint Laurent Rive Gauche, spring–summer 1967.

Sketch by Yves Saint Laurent of a polka-dot-print crepe dress with fringe, Saint Laurent Rive Gauche, spring–summer 1968.

Sketch by Yves Saint Laurent of a wool gabardine coat, Saint Laurent Rive Gauche, autumn–winter 1968.

Sketch by Yves Saint Laurent of a double-breasted wool coat, Saint Laurent Rive Gauche, autumn–winter 1968.

Sketch by Yves Saint Laurent of a whipcord coat, Saint Laurent Rive Gauche, spring–summer 1968.

Sketch by Yves Saint Laurent of a long dress in printed cotton poplin, Saint Laurent Rive Gauche, spring–summer 1968.

Sketch by Yves Saint Laurent of a jersey dress, Saint Laurent Rive Gauche, autumn–winter 1969.

Sheet of drawings, Saint Laurent
Rive Gauche, autumn–winter 1966.

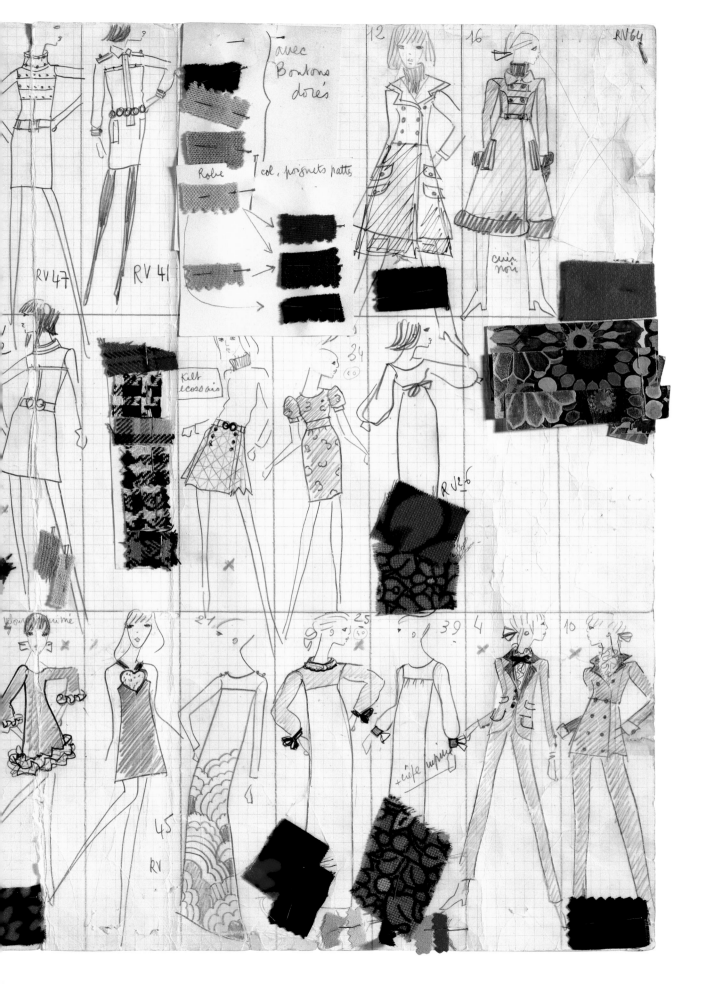

avec
Boutons
dorés

Robe

col, poignets pattes

RV 47

RV 41

RV 64

cuir noir

RV 26

Kilt
écossais

34

21 25 39 4 10

45

RV

67

Sheet of drawings, Saint Laurent
Rive Gauche, spring–summer 1967.

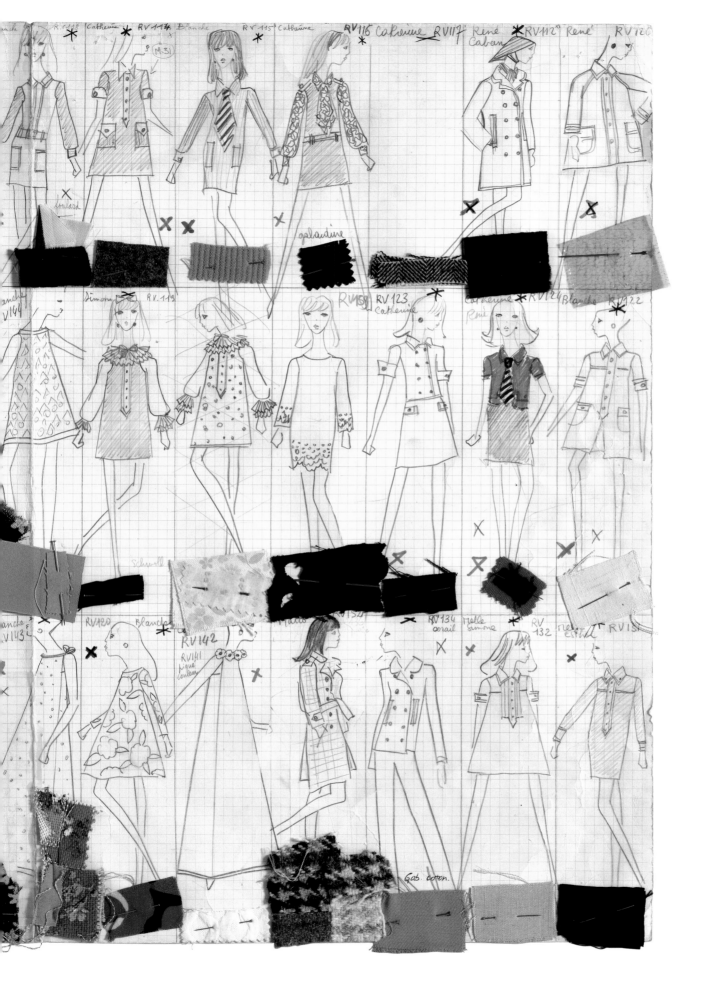

Sheet of drawings, Saint Laurent
Rive Gauche, spring–summer 1968.

RV397   RV323   RV322   RV321   RV330   RV329   RV367

RV361   RV335   RV163   RV125   RV368   RV377

RV352   RV354   RV355   RV353   RV355   RV378

CATHERINE DENEUVE, JEUNE FEMME MODÈLE

Ces mannequins dans la vitrine de Saint-Laurent rive gauche ne sont pas de cire. Le couturier — en trompe-l'œil sur le mur — a dédoublé pour nous Catherine Deneuve qui nous présente ainsi deux des nouveaux modèles de la collection boutique Saint-Laurent. **A gauche** : robe cravatée de surah imprimé tabac et noir comme les manches. **A droite** : robe en toile jaune à broderie mexicaine.
(**Reportage de Viviane CH.-GREYMOUR - Photographie de J.-P. CHEVALLIER.**)

Catherine Deneuve in a dress with sleeves made of the same black and brown fabric as the necktie (left) and a yellow linen dress with Mexican embroidery (right), Saint Laurent Rive Gauche, spring–summer 1967.
Le Figaro, February 12, 1967.
Photograph by J.-P. Chevallier.

Opposite:
Cotton piqué dress with guipure (detail), Saint Laurent Rive Gauche, spring–summer 1967.
Photograph by Sophie Carre.

A CERTAIN WAY OF LIVING RATHER THAN A CERTAIN WAY OF DRESSING.

YVES SAINT LAURENT, *DIM DAM DOM*, MARCH 10, 1968

Page 74: A pea jacket in gypsy-blue wool (detail), Saint Laurent Rive Gauche. Photograph by Sophie Carre.

Left: A double-breasted coat in wool cloth, Saint Laurent Rive Gauche, autumn–winter 1966.

A striped knit dress with a metal-ring belt, Saint Laurent Rive Gauche, autumn–winter 1966.

A wool
jersey dress,
Saint Laurent
Rive Gauche,
autumn–winter
1966.

A leather coat
with frogging,
Saint Laurent
Rive Gauche,
autumn–winter
1966.

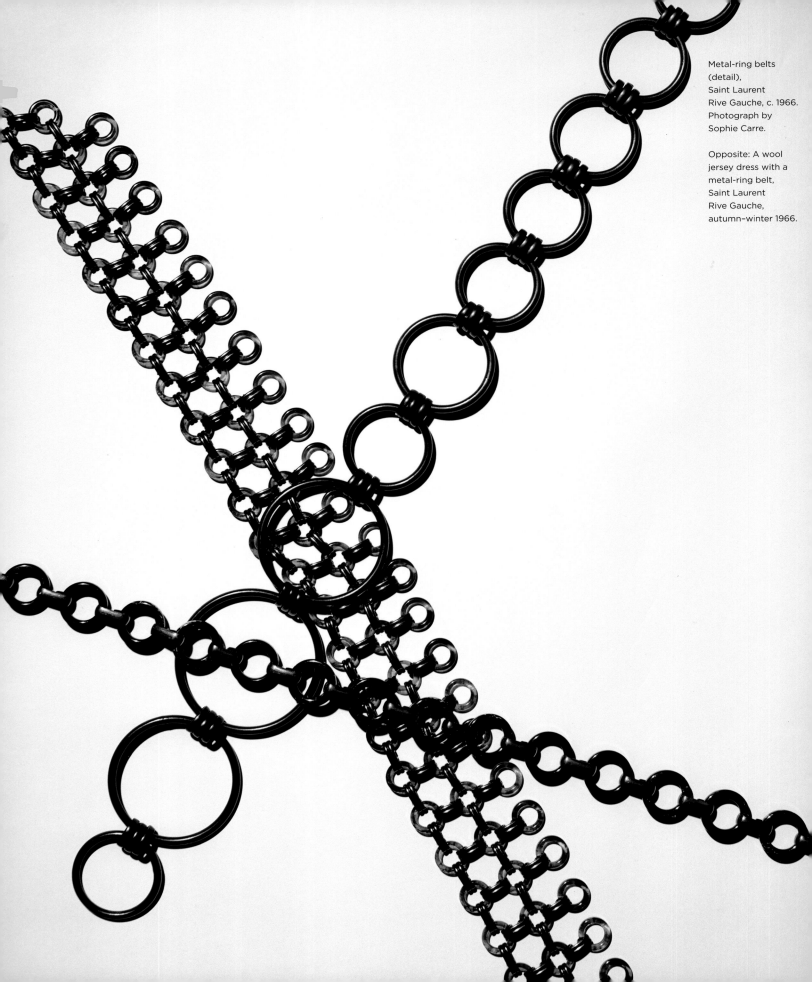

Metal-ring belts
(detail),
Saint Laurent
Rive Gauche, c. 1966.
Photograph by
Sophie Carre.

Opposite: A wool
jersey dress with a
metal-ring belt,
Saint Laurent
Rive Gauche,
autumn–winter 1966.

Left: Dresses in silk
shantung with neckties
in silk twill,
Saint Laurent
Rive Gauche,
spring–summer 1967.
French *Elle*,
March 23, 1967.
Photograph by
Just Jaeckin.

Opposite: A satchel
in blue denim and
leather (detail),
Saint Laurent
Rive Gauche,
spring–summer 1970.
Photograph by
Sophie Carre.

"WHEN YOU SEE A YVES SAINT LAURENT ELSEWHERE . . . SEE IF BEYOND HER PANTS FALL OF A STEREO CONVENTION, THE EX RHYTHM AND MOVE

FROM A PROFILE OF YVES SAINT LAURENT BY PHILIPPE LABRO, *LE JOURNAL DU DIMANCHE*, FEBRUARY 2, 1969

WOMAN WEARING
IN THE STREET . . . OR
YOU CAN'T MAKE OUT,
OR HER SUIT, THE
TYPE, THE END OF A
PRESSION OF THE
MENT OF OUR TIME."

ELLE

N° 1341

spécial Collections

2,50 F. GDE-BRETAGNE : 23 P. · SUISSE 2 FR. S. · U.S.A. : 60 CTS · CANADA : 60 CTS · ITALIE : 350 LIRES · ESPAGNE : 35 PTS · SUEDE : SKR. 3,75 INKL. MOMS · 30 AOUT 1971

Opposite: French
Elle, August 30, 1971.
Photograph by
Peter Knapp.

Left: An acces-
sorized ensemble,
Saint Laurent
Rive Gauche,
autumn–winter 1971.
French *Elle*,
August 30, 1971.
Photograph by
Peter Knapp.

Left: A dress in silk
shantung with a scarf
in silk twill,
Saint Laurent
Rive Gauche,
spring–summer 1967.
French *Elle*,
March 21, 1967.
Photograph by
André Carrara.

Opposite: An article
featuring French
ready-to-wear designs
in a Japanese setting,
including a white
Kalgan sheepskin coat
with black frogging
from Saint Laurent
Rive Gauche.
French *Vogue*, December
1967.
Photograph by
Peter Knapp.

Le passé : une rue encore entièrement pavée à l'ancienne, à gauche, qui mène au temple Hoshun-in à Kyoto, et des ombrelles en toile huilée. Le présent, ci-dessus : la toute dernière voiture sport, le coupé blanc Toyota, 2 000 G.T.

Manteau et capuchon, *à gauche*, en vison black Canada Majestic et fines bandes de cuir. André Sauzaie, 7 500 F. *Ci-dessus*, manteau en kalgan blanc à brandebourgs noirs. Saint Laurent Rive Gauche, 1 800 F et cuissardes en ginza et cuir, Charles Jourdan, en vente au Grand Magasin Seibu à Tokyo. Où trouver ces modèles ? **Voir page IX.**

NOTRE PRÊT-A-PORTER AU JAPON

21

An accessorized ensemble,
Saint Laurent Rive Gauche,
autumn–winter 1971. British
Vogue, October 1971.
Photograph by Arthur Elgort.

Left: A dress in printed
viscose crepe,
Saint Laurent
Rive Gauche,
spring–summer 1973.

Opposite:
Bodices in printed
cotton satin (detail),
Saint Laurent
Rive Gauche,
spring–summer 1969.
Photograph by
Sophie Carre.

Left and opposite:
British *Vogue*,
May 1971.
Photographs by
Jean-Jacques Buga

Saint Laurent in light summer vein- royal and dotty crepe

Here the Saints go dancing by—
bright frills, dotty prints,
dancing lengths.
Can this be strict Saint Laurent?
The only black is a belt,
a pair of wedge sandals;
all the rest are new summer
cottons, crepes, voiles,
poppied like so many hay fields,
spotted with colour,
put with brilliant legs
and purple espadrilles.
Flocks of red hearts, *left*,
on a white voile
drawstring blouse
and midi skirt
with stitched pleats over hips.
Raglan sleeves puffed to elbows.
£60.90. Red and black
plastic hearts love-locked
to black cord belt, £22.40.
Poppy choker, £12.20.
Dotted patch print crepe dress,
right, shirt top
with full sleeves gathered
into band above elbows,
stitched pleats from waist,
let go to cover the knee. £68.60.
Appliqué poppy belt, £10.75.
Patent wedge sandals,
on both pages, about £14.
Tights, £2.75. All from
Saint Laurent Rive Gauche.
Poppies in the hair,
by Novelty Import.
Hair by Oliver of Leonard

BUGAT

left bank flowers

left bank flowers

Left and opposite:
British *Vogue*, May
1971.
Photographs by
Jean-Jacques Bugat

Saint Laurent cottons in frills, tucks and full flower

Yellow cotton, *left*, sprinkled
with a dolly mixture print,
shiny black buttons
from V neck, puffed shoulders,
and stitched tucks from waist
let go into two frills,
short and sweet. £53.60.
Heavy cord silk belt,
clasped with a pair
of hearts in scarlet
and black plastic; £22.40.
Purple ribbed cotton vest,
right, inside a tied red cotton
shirt and tucked cotton skirt
to calf, flowered
with nasturtium colours.
Vest, £8.50, speckled shirt,
£12.90, skirt, about £25.
Purple wedged espadrilles, £8.90.
Lacquered poppy hairslide, £6.50.
Buttercup tights, £2.75.
All from Saint Laurent
Rive Gauche, New Bond St.
Buttercups in hair,. *left*,
extra flowers, by Novelty Import.
Lipstick, Charles of the Ritz
Rusticana Red.
Hair by Oliver of Leonard

BUGAT

LUXURY TODAY IS TO BE ALIVE, AND A WOMAN IS NOT ALIVE WHEN SHE IS WRAPPED IN CONSTRAINTS.

YVES SAINT LAURENT, AUGUST 1965

A loden cape and
wool jersey jumpsuit,
Saint Laurent
Rive Gauche,
autumn–winter 1969.
French *Vogue*,
September 1969.
Photograph by
Jeanloup Sieff.

Left: An ensemble in
woolen broadcloth with
a high-collared Eton
jacket with frogging,
Saint Laurent
Rive Gauche,
autumn–winter 1969.
French *Vogue*,
September 1969.
Photograph by
Jeanloup Sieff.

Opposite:
A kid-leather blouse
and a tweed skirt,
Saint Laurent
Rive Gauche,
autumn–winter 1969.
French *Vogue*,
September 1969.
Photograph by
Jeanloup Sieff.

I AM MOVING TOWARD GREATER RIGOR . . . MY GOAL IS TO DEVELOP PROTOTYPES THAT WILL NOT GO OUT OF FASHION. LIKE JEANS, WHICH HAVE REACHED PERFECTION.

YVES SAINT LAURENT, FRENCH *VOGUE*, FEBRUARY 1973

A blue denim suit,
Saint Laurent
Rive Gauche,
spring–summer 1970.

Right: A blue denim suit, Saint Laurent Rive Gauche, spring–summer 1970. French *Vogue*, February 1970. Photograph by Jeanloup Sieff.

Opposite: A suit in black cotton satin, Saint Laurent Rive Gauche, spring–summer 1970. French *Vogue*, February 1970. Photograph by Jeanloup Sieff.

A la source un
créateur ; un lancement raz-de-marée ; et
31 boutiques dispersées dans le
monde pour propager l'inondation : Yves
Saint Laurent, aidé d'une
organisation industrielle et
commerciale à citer en modèle va
parachuter ce printemps une
mode toute neuve, à des prix imbattables.

A gauche : en jeans, un tailleur
cintré, à longues basques, sur une jupe
à mi-mollet. Saint Laurent-Rive Gauche.
F 380. Serre-cou en soie noire.

A droite : toujours cintré,
en satin de coton noir, un tailleur
à boutons bottines et longues
basques sur jupe à mi-mollet.
Saint Laurent-Rive Gauche.
F 450. Coiffures Carita.
Adresses page 17.

LE GRAND SAINT LAURENT

JEANLOUP SIEFF

71

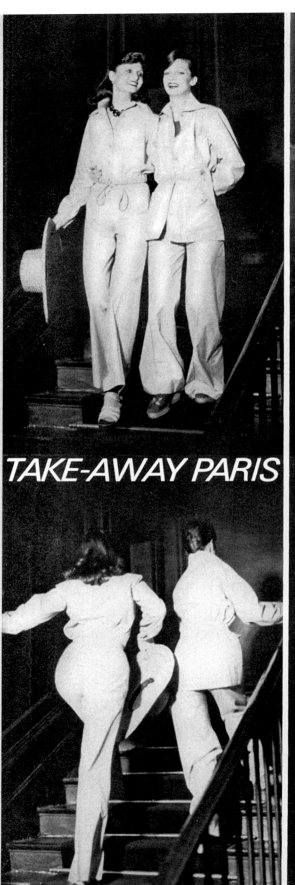
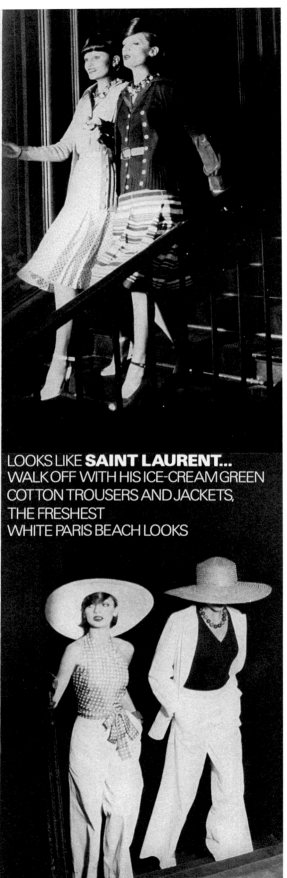

Near right:
Pistachio
battle jacket
and Oxford bags,
the trousers on
drawstring waist;
£27·75, £11.
Black plastic
necklace, £11.
Rope sandals, £14.
Safari jacket
bloused onto
inset waistband,
wide trousers,
soft donkey brown
T-shirt sweater;
£30, £17, £7·50.
Brown appliquéd
espadrilles, £11.
*Opposite, and below
second right:*
Loose white
trousers,
tight wrap bodice
of green and white
taffeta checks;
£15, £24.
Cream straw hat.
White patent
shoes, £25.
Long loose jacket
and wide trousers
in cotton,
all the whiter
for thin navy
V-neck sweater
inside; £39, £15,
£13·75. Pistachio
straw hat.
Plastic necklace.
Clothes,
top second right:
second view and
details *overleaf.*
All clothes
from Saint Laurent
Rive Gauche.
Hair by Jean-Louis
Davide, Paris

TAKE-AWAY PARIS

LOOKS LIKE **SAINT LAURENT…**
WALK OFF WITH HIS ICE-CREAM GREEN
COTTON TROUSERS AND JACKETS,
THE FRESHEST
WHITE PARIS BEACH LOOKS

PETER KNAPP

Opposite:
British *Vogue*,
March 1972.
Photograph by
Peter Knapp.

Right: Edie Baskin
wearing an ensemble
by Saint Laurent
Rive Gauche for men,
spring–summer 1976.
American *Vogue*,
January 1976.
Photograph by
Berry Berenson.

Opposite:
Françoise Hardy in a
crepe de chine shirt,
a wool knit vest,
velvet breeches, a belt
with enameled buckle,
and lace-up boots,
Saint Laurent
Rive Gauche,
autumn–winter 1970.
Photograph by
Arnaud de Rosnay.

Right: A cotton
gabardine trench
coat, Saint Laurent
Rive Gauche,
autumn–winter 1970.
French *Elle*, January
19, 1970.
Photograph by
Elisabeth Novick.

Left: A long
sheepskin jacket
over a dress in
printed muslin,
Saint Laurent
Rive Gauche,
autumn–winter 1971.
French *Elle*, June 9,
1971.
Photograph by
Hans Feurer.

Opposite:
A necklace over
a scarf (detail),
Saint Laurent
Rive Gauche, 1970s.
Photograph by
Sophie Carre.

I TRY TO TRANSLATE A BODILY ATTITUDE AND, IN THE END, A MORAL ATTITUDE: THE FREEDOM AND OPEN-MINDEDNESS OF A WOMAN.

YVES SAINT LAURENT, FEBRUARY 1969

A jacket in cotton poplin,
Saint Laurent
Rive Gauche,
autumn–winter 1972.
French *Marie Claire*,
February 1972.
Photograph by
Alex Chatelain.

A dress in rayon crepe
with leg-of-mutton
sleeves and cassock
buttons,
Saint Laurent
Rive Gauche,
spring–summer 1971.
French *Elle*,
May 10, 1971.
Photograph by
Peter Knapp.

A printed crepe
dress, Saint Laurent
Rive Gauche,
spring–summer 1972.
Italian *Vogue*,
June 1972.
Photograph by
Jeanloup Sieff.

MY DREAM IS TO MAKE THINGS THAT CAN BE MIXED TOGETHER: A COAT IS ONLY BEAUTIFUL, FOR ME, IF A WOMAN CAN BUY IT AND WEAR IT WITH ANYTHING.

YVES SAINT LAURENT, FEBRUARY 1969

A knee-length, pleated schoolgirl skirt in white flannel with a black wool blazer with white accents, Saint Laurent Rive Gauche, spring–summer 1971. French *Vogue*, March 1971. Photograph by Jeanloup Sieff.

La jupe plissée de lycéenne en flanelle blanche : elle est au genou. Elle se porte (à droite), sous un blazer croisé en lainage noir bordé blanc. Camélia à la boutonnière. Saint Laurent-Rive Gauche. Chaussures à talon haut. Yves Saint Laurent à la Bottique. Coiffures Dany de chez Camille Albane.

"SAINT LAURENT'S WOMEN CASTLES, EVEN SUBURBS STREETS, THE SUBWAYS, THE STOCK EXCHANGE."

MARGUERITE DURAS, "LE BRUIT ET LE SILENCE," SUMMER 1987

EMERGED FROM HAREMS, THEY ARE WALKING THE THE DEPARTMENT STORES,

Opposite: An ensemble in wool gabardine featuring a double-breasted jacket with belt and belt loops, and wide trousers, Saint Laurent Rive Gauche, spring–summer 1972. French *Elle*, February 28, 1972. Photograph by Hans Feurer.

Right, top: A checked wool blazer over a sailcloth blouse and gabardine skirt.

Right, bottom: A long, belted shirt in wool jersey, a silk blouse, and a bayadere crepe skirt, Saint Laurent Rive Gauche, spring–summer 1972. French *Elle*, March 13, 1972. Photographs by Marc Hispard.

Opposite: A cashmere
cardigan with a fox
collar (detail),
Saint Laurent
Rive Gauche,
autumn–winter 1973.
Photograph by
Sophie Carre.

Right: A cashmere
cardigan with a fox
collar paired with a
wraparound skirt in
tweed, Saint Laurent
Rive Gauche,
autumn–winter 1973.

Left: A belted dress
in printed crepe,
Saint Laurent
Rive Gauche,
spring–summer 1974.
British *Vogue*, April 1974.
Photograph by
Guy Bourdin.

Opposite: A belted
dress in polka-dot-print
crepe, Saint Laurent
Rive Gauche,
spring–summer 1974.
British *Vogue*, April 1974.
Photograph by
Guy Bourdin.

A dress in muslin and feathers, a muslin blouse and black crepe skirt, and a dress in muslin and lace. British *Vogue*, March 1977.
Photograph by Guy Bourdin.

Opposite: A black oilskin raincoat,
Saint Laurent Rive Gauche,
spring–summer 1973.
American *Vogue*, March 1973.
Photograph by Chris von Wangenheim.

Below: A belt in black cord and
galalithe (detail), Saint Laurent
Rive Gauche, spring–summer 1971.
Photograph by Sophie Carre.

CATHERINE DENEUVE
THE ONE HE WAS WAITING FOR. THE ONE SHE WAS WAITING FOR.

Catherine Deneuve in
a belted, sleeveless
jersey dress,
Saint Laurent
Rive Gauche,
autumn–winter 1966.
Photograph by
Reg Lancaster.

Right: Catherine Deneuve
in a black wool dress
edged with gold braid,
Saint Laurent Rive Gauche,
spring–summer 1967. British
Vogue, April 1967.
Photograph by David Bailey.

Opposite: Catherine
Deneuve in a cotton piqué
dress with guipure appliqué,
Saint Laurent Rive Gauche,
spring–summer 1967.
British *Vogue*, April 1967.
Photograph by David Bailey.

Opposite: A safari jacket in cotton cloth (detail), Saint Laurent Rive Gauche, spring–summer 1968. Photograph by Sophie Carre.

Right: An article showcasing the style of Saint Laurent Rive Gauche model Catherine Deneuve, highlighting her love of boots, no matter the outfit. *Paris Match*, October 24, 1970. Photographs by François Gragnon.

LA MODE DE CATHERINE
En maxi, en panta-court, en cape, en manteau, mais toujours en bottes

BETTY CATROUX

A CHILD DRESSED IN BLACK WHO RESEMBLED ME LIKE A BROTHER.

Betty Catroux and
Yves Saint Laurent
had a close bond,
often comparing
their relationship
to that of siblings
(see page 42).
Betty Catroux in a
long sleeveless tunic,
laced with a leather
thong, and matching
pants. French *Vogue*,
November 1968.
Photograph by
Jeanloup Sieff.

Opposite: Betty
Catroux in a poplin
jacket and pants,
Saint Laurent
Rive Gauche,
spring–summer 1969.
American *Vogue*,
March 1969.
Photograph by
Ewa Rudling.

Right: Betty Catroux
wearing a jumpsuit
in the Saint Laurent
Rive Gauche store at
38 rue du Faubourg
Saint-Honoré, Paris,
in 1969.
Photograph by
Peter Caine.

LOULOU DE LA FALAISE

HE IS THE ONE WHO MADE ME INTO A PARISIENNE.

EASY YVES, EASY DOES IT

Our choice of the new collection photographed in Paris and on sale now in London

What's in it for you with Saint Laurent today: Yves loves white and bright colours. Yves loves pants—especially wide ones— shirtdresses, pleats and cardigan jackets. Yves loves spots, stripes and checks. Yves loves high-heeled shoes and espadrilles. Yves loves bare back dresses for summer nights. Yves loves easy clothes. Yves loves you to look relaxed. So do we: so we feel, will you.

LOUISE de la FALAISE is the model and one of Yves best friends. She is like quick silver, always laughing, always on the move. She's got star-quality style and glamour. Half French and half English she's been a designer, a dancer, a model and a fashion editor. She flits between Paris, London and New York and is at home in all three. "Now I'm working for Yves I'll be based more and more in Paris. What I love about this new collection is that all the clothes are so easy, so relaxed."

Page 141: British *Flair*, March 1975.

Right: Loulou de la Falaise with Yves Saint Laurent seated on a sheep by François-Xavier Lalanne.
Loulou de la Falaise is wearing a dress in printed crepe, Saint Laurent Rive Gauche, French *Vogue*, March 1975.
Photograph by Uli Rose.

LES BOUTIQUES DE VOGUE

L'ART DE MÉLANGER LES TROUVAILLES OU COMMENT DEVENIR SON PROPRE COUTURIER

- "**Ma mère voulait que je sois poète... alors elle m'a appelée *Louise*.**"

- "J'aime le présent, la jeunesse de maintenant.. je me sens en accord avec la jeunesse anglaise... pas la française..."
- "L'atmosphère de Londres, c'est ce que je préfère... J'aimerais vivre six mois à la campagne en Angleterre, dans une grande maison, et six mois au Maroc, peu importe le temps de l'année..."

- *"Ce qui m'amuse, c'est de prendre une fille mal habillée mais jolie, et de lui dire ce qu'elle doit faire. J'aimerais réaliser quelques idées que j'ai depuis longtemps..."*

- "**IL FAUT CROIRE AUX FANTOMES POUR EN VOIR... J'EN AI VU...**"
"Je n'aime pas tellement le rouge, le bleu marine..."

- "On a toujours eu des complexes envers nos mères..."
Louise se trouve moins jolie que sa mère, qui se trouve moins jolie que Lady Birley, qui se trouve moins jolie que ne l'était sa mère.

Louise Fitz-Gérald de la Falaise *est la petite fille du peintre Oswald Birley. Grands yeux écartés des rêveurs, longues mains des poètes. Seule loi : la fantaisie. Plus intéressée par les accessoires que par la mode elle-même,* **Louise** *s'habille de "riens" dénichés au cours de ses voyages. De tempérament artiste, elle a le talent de savoir les choisir, une manière à elle de les réunir. Avec habileté, elle sait comment draper n'importe quel tissu en turban, y fixer un dragon, un papillon (ci-dessus). Sa beauté est romanesque, chaque jour différente. Imitez son génie du colifichet.*

Ses goûts ?
Rossetti, Burn Jones,
Beardsley, Klimt...

*Elle est elle-même un Gustave Moreau, un Odilon Redon. Ensemble-pantalon en tissu japonais moletonné, imprimé de dragons et de bouquets de violettes. **Ossie Clark,** Quorum, 52, Radnor Walk. Londres. Sur la tête, une soie noire enserre les cheveux. Au cou, écharpe 1930 du Antique Market, Kingsroad, Londres. Ceinture d'argent du Marché aux Puces, Paris. Bottes de Saint Laurent-Rive Gauche.*

- Un peu fée

*un peu 1930... "comme tout ce que fait **Ossie Clark".** Mis en valeur par **Louise** dansant sur son lit, ensemble arachnéen, absolument extraordinaire de légèreté, d'imprévu, de jamais vu.*

Ses colliers

*Ceux qui ne servent pas sont suspendus au mur. Douée du sens des couleurs, **Louise** mélange ambre, corail de Téroudan, chaîne victorienne et pierres bleues. Au poignet, serre-nappe volé au "Petit Saint-Père" ! Turban bleu-vert et orange piqué d'un dragon trouvé aux Puces.*

Le noir, je ne le porte qu'à Paris...

*... Paris, pour moi, c'est six personnes et la place Furstenberg..." dit **Louise** dans une tenue subtile où contrastent tous les noirs. Velours de l'ensemble-pantalon évasé de Saint Laurent-Rive Gauche, soie du turban drapé à la manière des femmes du sud marocain, colliers de jais, perles d'acier et passementerie de perles grises que portent les gondoliers à Venise.*

PATRICK SAUTERET

Beauty for All

Gilles de Bure

To look at the river made of time and water
And remember that time is another river,
To know that we are lost like the river
And that faces dissolve like water.
—Jorge Luis Borges, "Ars Poetica"

There are faces, though, that are never erased however much time passes. It is tempting to follow Borges with a quote from Frédéric Fajardie, who, writing about the 1960s, said: "We flowed happy days…"

The 1960s started off with a bang. In 1963, three young women began work on a practical revolution whose effects would only be measured much later. Two former models, Christiane Bailly and Emmanuelle Khanh, started the label Emma Christie, while a former reporter, Michèle Rosier, reinvented the V de V (Vêtements de Vacance) collections. Between the three of them, they launched a new idea, the idea of "style," which would be taken up and popularized by two politically engaged women's magazines, *Elle* and *Jardin des Modes*. The three adventuresses shared an assistant, Paco Rabanne, then still an architecture student, and a "little hand" with skillful fingers, Azzedine Alaïa.

The following year, Terence Conran opened his first Habitat store in London—its mission was also to change the look of everyday life in the West. Beauty for everyone, everywhere, and at every moment, said the three Parisian women and the Londoner. That same year, Aimé Maeght opened his foundation's doors in Saint-Paul-de-Vence in a spectacular building by the architect Josep Lluís Sert, and Robert Rauschenberg won the Grand Prize at the Venice Biennale. Art was suddenly taking its place

147

in the public arena. In 1965, a heated war of words flared up between London and Paris: Mary Quant and André Courrèges each claimed to have invented the miniskirt, which appeared at the same time as panty hose. And in the meantime, Denise Fayolle was inventing the Prisunic style, putting together a catalog for the department store that included designs by Gae Aulenti, Terence Conran, and Marc Held and offering bargain-priced lithographs chosen by Andrée Putman and signed by Pierre Alechinsky, Reinhoud d'Haese, Henry van de Velde, and others.

A few years later, in 1968, Maïmé Arnodin, Denise Fayolle, Antoine Kieffer (former artistic director of *Vogue*), Andrée Putman, and Claude Thiriet would create Mafia (Maïmé Arnodin, Fayolle, International Associates) and would handle, for a time, the advertising for Saint Laurent Rive Gauche.

Yves Saint Laurent had presented an extraordinary collection in 1965 in homage to Mondrian and Serge Poliakoff. Later would come homages to Picasso, Tom Wesselmann, Jean Cocteau, and Georges Braque; but already Saint Laurent was erasing boundaries, mixing genres, telescoping stylistic expressions, and imagining design in all its forms. "I have always put a respect for the metier ahead of everything else, which, though it is not quite an art, requires an artist to exist," said Saint Laurent. Nabokov comes to mind here, who said: "Art, that lunatic magician who puts lipstick on the lips of life."

In a parallel development, the human sciences were starting to occupy the front row in the windows of bookstores. In 1964, Claude Lévi-Strauss published his masterpiece *The Raw and the Cooked*. In 1965, he put the finishing touches on the second volume of his *Mythologiques*, published in 1967 as *From Honey to Ashes*. This general territory attracted many writers in the 1960s. Among other works published in the lead-up to May 1968 were Jacques Lacan's *Écrits* and Michel Foucault's *The Order of Things*, both in 1966; Guy Debord's *The Society of the Spectacle* and Raoul Vaneigem's *The Revolution of Everyday Life*, both in 1967; and Jean Baudrillard's *The System of Objects* in early 1968.

Yves Saint Laurent in front of the Saint Laurent Rive Gauche store at 21 rue de Tournon, Paris, on September 26, 1966, with a model wearing a suede calfskin skirt and striped shetland sweater, Saint Laurent Rive Gauche, autumn–winter 1966.

These events might seem to have been happening at some distance from one another. Yet all these battle steeds were advancing at the same pace.

In January 1966, Fidel Castro organized the first Tricontinental Conference in Havana, which was intended to create a network of revolutionary solidarity between the peoples of Africa, Latin America, and Asia. More than five hundred delegates responded to his invitation.

The civil rights movement was heating up in the United States. Black Power became a watchword, and the Black Panthers its militant expression. The first hippie communes appeared in California, while China was torn apart by its Cultural Revolution.

In New York, Betty Friedan founded the National Organization for Women, which was followed in 1967 by the Women's Liberation Movement. All of these organizations and movements shared one thing in common, which was an insistence on autonomy, identity, and difference. The year 1966 was also rich in cultural offerings. Authors were being translated from page to screen in quick succession: Denis Diderot, for example, in Jacques Rivette's *The Nun*; Robert Musil in Volker Schlöndorff's *The Confusions of Young Törless*; Boris Pasternak in David Lean's *Doctor Zhivago*; Ray Bradbury in François Truffaut's *Fahrenheit 451*; and José Giovanni in Jean-Pierre Melville's *Second Breath*.

In Paris theaters, Françoise Sagan was represented, with *L'Écharde* and *Le Cheval Évanoui*; Jean Genet with *The Screens*; and Peter Weiss with *Marat/Sade*. At the Théâtre des Champs-Élysées, Roland Petit staged his *In Praise of Folly*, after the classic text by Erasmus, to music of Marius Constant, with sets by Martial Raysse, Niki de Saint-Phalle, and Jean Tinguely, and with Zizi Jeanmaire in the spotlight. Sagan and Jeanmaire were, as always, members of the Saint Laurent nebula.

In music, 1966 was the year that the Beatles gave their last concert, on April 29 in San Francisco, and also the year that Pink Floyd was formed. At the same time, Jean-Claude Malgoire was founding his period-instrument

The Saint Laurent Rive Gauche store at 21 rue de Tournon, Paris.

ensemble, La Grande Écurie et la Chambre du Roy, and Steve Reich was inventing his phase music, which has come to be lumped with the minimalists.

Contemporary architecture, for its part, lagged behind the other arts, despite the start of construction on Minoru Yamasaki's World Trade Center in New York in 1972. Its expression took the form of utopian projects, conceived by cooperatives of young people who dreamed communally and mixed technology with comic books: Archizoom and Superstudio in Florence, Archigram in London, and AJS Aérolande in Paris are its most prominent examples.

These great movements that were shaking the world did not go unnoticed by Yves Saint Laurent. As someone who absorbed the world to an uncommon degree, a "celestial sponge," as Jack Kerouac might have said, he sensed that the world was tipping into another configuration. He had already democratized the tuxedo and planned to domesticate the pea jacket and the safari jacket, saying: "If I have a regret, it is that I did not invent blue jeans." His thinking ran to "style rather than fashion," and he would tell Claude Berthod that he was looking for "a certain way of living rather than a certain way of dressing" (*Dim Dam Dom,* March 10, 1968).

On September 26, 1966, he took the plunge. A giant stride brought him from rue Spontini to rue de Tournon in the heart of the sixth arrondissement, within a stone's throw of the Luxembourg Gardens. Saint Laurent Rive Gauche was wide open. At that time, the words "Rive Gauche" still carried their full weight. The Left Bank suggested and was in fact identified with philosophical thought and artistic creation, the world of literature, a certain bohemianism, the university, and jazz. In short, the Left Bank still frightened and amazed the Right Bank. At 21 rue de Tournon, formerly a bakery then an antique store, the premises had lain vacant for years. Long and narrow, the shop led tunnel-like toward a tiny garden in the back. The task at hand was to make it extraordinary. Powerful but not showy. To respect the spirit of the Left Bank, and at the same time to go beyond it, to take it further.

Yves Saint Laurent and Pierre Bergé called on Isabelle Hebey for help. An interior designer who had studied psychology and sociology as well as

The Saint Laurent Rive Gauche store at 21 rue de Tournon, Paris.

153

the history of art, Hebey had an acute sense of the rhythms of the time, its fashions and mores. At rue de Tournon, she would juxtapose with much subtlety, chicness, and modernity the traditionalism of couture with the innovation of current fashion, using raw materials (exposed stone and wooden beams) and highly polished materials (glass and aluminum). A foot on each bank of the Seine, as it were. Oxblood was the dominant color, both for the carpeting and the open-worked metal screens. On the walls there was a full-length portrait of Yves Saint Laurent by the very young Eduardo Arroyo with pieces by Andy Warhol and Tom Wesselmann scattered about. Punctuating the space were paper lamps by the Japanese American sculptor Isamu Noguchi, discovered at Steph Simon's next door, and wave-shaped Djinn hassocks by Olivier Mourgue covered in violet jersey (two years later, Stanley Kubrick would furnish the lobby of his outer-space Hilton in *2001: A Space Odyssey* with the same Djinn seating). In the garden were a few small "Nanas" by Niki de Saint-Phalle.

The whole created a startling effect, one of extraordinary freedom, measured insouciance, and triumphant youth. A happy and unrestrained meeting ground, a sophisticated souk, like a Marrakech temptation.

The Saint Laurent Rive Gauche store had many imitators and did much for the career of Isabelle Hebey, who resurfaced not at the controls of but as the interior designer for the McDonnell Douglas DC-10 (1970), the Airbus (1971), and the Concorde (1972). Much later, in 1986, she would decorate the Élysée Palace office of First Lady Danielle Mitterrand.

During the eventful year of 1966, these small precincts on the Left Bank were vibrant with activity. Radicalized Parisians marched to the nearby Odéon Theater, where Jean Genet's *The Screens*—a critical look at the French-Algerian War directed by Roger Blin—was causing controversy, while everyone in Paris who sang and danced made their pilgrimage to rue de Tournon, a location that reveals Saint Laurent Rive Gauche's place at the center of this revolutionary era of creativity and change.

Above: Yves Saint Laurent and three models
with a sculpture by Niki de Saint-Phalle in
the courtyard of the rue de Tournon store,
September 26, 1966.
Photograph by Alain Nogues.

Overleaf: Yves Saint Laurent in front of his
portrait by Eduardo Arroyo, September 26,
1966.
Photograph by Reg Lancaster.

I TELL MYSELF THAT I HAVE NOT GOTTEN FAR ENOUGH AWAY FROM FASHION, FROM HAUTE COUTURE, AND I HOPE THAT THIS FIELD WILL CHANGE EVEN MORE PROFOUNDLY . . . THAT THE STEREOTYPES WILL EXPLODE, AS THEY HAVE IN EVERY OTHER DOMAIN.

YVES SAINT LAURENT, FEBRUARY 1969

Photography credits and copyrights

Front cover © Wesley / Keystone / Getty Images
p. 7 © Meerson
pp. 12–13 © Yoshida / *Elle* / SCOOP
p. 17 © Marie Cosindas / Courtesy of HP Garcia Gallery, NYC
p. 21 © Alain Nogues / Sygma / Corbis
p. 22 © Jean-Jacques Bugat / Condé Nast Archive © Condé Nast Publications
p. 25 © Sophie Carre
p. 29 © Fondation Pierre Bergé–Yves Saint Laurent
pp. 30–31 © *Women's Wear Daily*
p. 33 © Sophie Carre
pp. 38–41 © Publifoto / P.-L. Thiessard / Michaël Doster / Pierre Burdin / Marc Fabre / Peter Caine / Omaggio / Danièle Suissa / Lo Studio / Ingrid V. Senger / Martha Holmes / French *Vogue*
p. 43 © Wesley / Keystone / Getty Images
pp. 45, 46, 48, and 49 © The Estate of Jeanloup Sieff
p. 53 © Sophie Carre
pp. 54–57 © Henri Elwing / *Elle* / SCOOP
pp. 58–59 © David Bailey / *Elle* / SCOOP
pp. 61–71 © Fondation Pierre Bergé–Yves Saint Laurent
p. 72 Text © Viviane Ch. Greymour / *Le Figaro* / 1967
Photo © J.-P. Chevallier / *Le Figaro* / 1967
pp. 73–74 © Sophie Carre
p. 80 © Sophie Carre
p. 82 © Just Jaeckin / *Elle* / SCOOP
p. 83 © Sophie Carre
pp. 86–87 © Peter Knapp / *Elle* / SCOOP
p. 88 © André Carrara / *Elle* / SCOOP
p. 89 © Peter Knapp / French *Vogue*
pp. 90–91 © Arthur Elgort
p. 93 © Sophie Carre
pp. 94–97 Jean-Jacques Bugat / *Vogue* © Condé Nast Publications
pp. 99–101 © The Estate of Jeanloup Sieff
pp. 104–105 © The Estate of Jeanloup Sieff
p. 106 Peter Knapp / *Vogue* © Condé Nast Publications

p. 107 © Condé Nast Archive / Corbis
p. 108 Arnaud de Rosnay / Condé Nast Archive © Condé Nast Publications
p. 109 © Elisabeth Novick / *Elle* / SCOOP
p. 110 © Hans Feurer / *Elle* / SCOOP
p. 111 © Sophie Carre
p. 113 © Alex Chatelain / SIC
p. 114 © Peter Knapp / *Elle* / SCOOP
pp. 115 and 117 © The Estate of Jeanloup Sieff
p. 120 © Hans Feurer / *Elle* / SCOOP
p. 121 © Marc Hispard / *Elle* / SCOOP
p. 122 © Sophie Carre
pp. 124–127 © The Estate of Guy Bourdin
Guy Bourdin / *Vogue* © Condé Nast Publications
p. 128 Chris von Wangenheim / Condé Nast Archive © Condé Nast Publications
p. 129 © Sophie Carre
p. 131 © Reg Lancaster / Hulton / Getty Images
pp. 132–133 David Bailey / *Vogue* © Condé Nast Publications
p. 134 © Sophie Carre
p. 135 © François Gragnon / *Paris Match* / SCOOP
p. 137 © The Estate of Jeanloup Sieff
p. 138 Ewa Rudling / Condé Nast Archive © Condé Nast Publications
p. 139 © Peter Caine
p. 143 © Uli Rose
pp. 144–145 © Patrick Sauteret / French *Vogue*
p. 148 © Keystone France
p. 155 © Alain Nogues / Sygma / Corbis
p. 156 © Reg Lancaster / Hulton / Getty Images
Back cover © International Center of Photography, David Seidner Archive

To our considerable regret, we have been unable to publish any photographs by Helmut Newton, a great artist who worked for many years with Yves Saint Laurent.

This work was published in conjunction with the exhibition organized by the Fondation Pierre Bergé-Yves Saint Laurent

Saint Laurent Rive Gauche
La révolution de la mode

on view from March 5 to July 17, 2011, in its space on avenue Marceau, Paris.

Chief curator of the exhibition: **Pierre Bergé**
Artistic director: **Loulou de la Falaise**
Consultant: **Dominique Deroche**
Exhibition design: **Christophe Martin**

Pierre Bergé extends his heartfelt thanks to all who contributed to the making of this exhibition and catalog.

Lenders to the exhibition
Anouschka, Alyne de Broglie, Betty Catroux, Olivier Chatenet, Anne-Marie Colban, Loulou de la Falaise, Didier Ludot, Anne-Marie Muñoz, Ariel de Ravenel, and Mary Russell

Authors of the catalog
Jéromine Savignon and Gilles de Bure

Conservators and curators at the Foundation
Sophie Couret, Laurence Neveu, Mireille Prulhière, Catherine Zeitoun, Violaine Blaise, and Émile Énard

Foundation archives and documentation
Sandrine Tinturier, Catherine Gadala, Kamel Khemissi, and Pauline Vidal

Foundation registrars
Valérie Mulattieri and Joséphine Théry

Foundation communications
Laetitia Roux, Olivier Flaviano, and Andréa Longrais

At the Musée Galliera—Musée de la Mode de la Ville de Paris
Sylvie Roy, Nathalie Gourseau, Dominique Revellino, and Jacqueline Dumaine

At the Musée des Arts Décoratifs
Christelle Di Giovanni, Caroline Pinon, and Marie-Pierre Ribère

As well as
Caroline Berton, Vanessa Bernard and French *Vogue*, Samuel Bourdin, Marie Cosindas, Nelly Douthaut and the Scoop Agency, Hughes de Pagan Garcia, Uli Rose, the heirs of Arnaud de Rosnay, Barbara Sieff, Shelly Verthime, and Sylvie Zameczkowski-Jardin

At the Fondation Pierre Bergé-Yves Saint Laurent
Philippe Mugnier, Olivier Ségot, and Pascal Sittler

At Éditions de la Martinière
Isabelle Jendron, Brigitte Govignon, Isabelle Dartois, Cécile Vandenbroucque, Éric Peyronnet, and Colette Malandain

Graphic design
Alexandre Wolkoff, with Camille Verkinderen, the Wolkoff and Arnodin Agency

Photographer
Sophie Carre

Jéromine Savignon extends her special thanks to Pierre Bergé for guiding her—in complete freedom—to the heart of the Saint Laurent Rive Gauche adventure.
She also thanks the following for the valuable information they contributed: Claude Berthod, Claude Brouet, Gilles de Bure, Gabrielle Busschaert, Betty Catroux, Catherine Deneuve, Dominique Deroche, Pierre Dinand, Loulou de la Falaise, Marie-José Lepicard, Baroness Hélène de Ludinghausen, Franka de Mailly, Philippe Mugnier, Anne-Marie Muñoz, Ariel de Ravenel, Mariella Righini, Clara Saint, Susan Train, and Connie Uzzo.

Fondation Pierre Bergé-Yves Saint Laurent
Board of directors

ABOUT THE CONTRIBUTORS

Pierre Bergé, born in 1930, became interested in literature at a young age, founding the review *La Patrie Mondiale*. For eight years, he managed the work of his friend, the painter Bernard Buffet, before diving into the fashion world with the very young and very talented Yves Saint Laurent, whom he met in 1958. Together they founded the Yves Saint Laurent fashion house in 1961. Pierre Bergé assumed the management and, over the years, built a luxury-goods empire for the YSL brand. In the 1980s, as a close friend of François Mitterrand, he started the weekly *Globe*. A committed activist, he supported the French antiracist organization SOS Racisme, chaired the AIDS organization Sidaction, advocated for gay rights by starting the magazine *Têtu*, and invested in Pink TV. Active in the theater as well, he was director of the Athénée Louis-Jouvet then of the Paris National Opera from 1988 to 1994, simultaneously working toward the opening of the Bastille Opera. In 2001, he founded the auction house Pierre Bergé and Associates. In 2002, Yves Saint Laurent and Pierre Bergé created the Fondation Pierre Bergé–Yves Saint Laurent, whose mission is to conserve and make known the work of Yves Saint Laurent, to organize exhibitions, and to support cultural projects in a variety of fields. In 2009, a year after Yves Saint Laurent's death, Pierre Bergé sold the fabulous collection of artworks they had gathered in tandem.

Today, he divides his time between the Foundation, of which he is president, the presidency of the oversight board of the *Le Monde* group, the Majorelle Garden in Marrakech, and Tangier, where he has bought the bookstore Librairie des Colonnes.

He is the author of several books, among them *Inventaire Mitterrand*, *Lettres à Yves*, and *Yves Saint Laurent: Une Passion Marocaine*.

Jéromine Savignon, a fashion historian, is the author of *Michael Jackson: The Auction* (with Arno Bani), *Jacques Fath*, *Jean-Louis Scherrer*, *Cacharel: Le Liberty*, and *L'Esprit Vionnet*. She has also written numerous articles, particularly on the fashion of the 1960s and 1970s, for a variety of catalogs and publications.

Gilles de Bure, a journalist and critic, is currently architecture editor of the *Journal des Arts*, and a contributor to *Keith* and *Numéro*. He is the author of some thirty books on art, architecture, photography, and design. The curator of numerous exhibitions, he was responsible for opening the Pompidou Center's contemporary-events gallery and was the first director of the Great Hall at La Villette.

FRENCH-LANGUAGE EDITION
Graphic design
Alexandre Wolkoff, with Camille Verkinderen
The Wolkoff and Arnodin Agency
Editing
Brigitte Govignon and Isabelle Dartois
Documentation and picture research
Sandrine Tinturier, Catherine Gadala, Kamel Khemissi, and Pauline Vidal
Copyediting and proofreading
Colette Malandain
Production
Éric Peyronnet

Translated from the French by Willard Wood

ENGLISH-LANGUAGE EDITION
Editor
Laura Dozier
Designer
Shawn Dahl, dahlimama inc
Production Manager
Jules Thomson

Library of Congress Cataloging-in-Publication Data
Savignon, Jéromine.
  Saint Laurent Rive Gauche : the fashion revolution / foreword by Pierre Bergé ; essays by Jéromine Savignon and Gilles de Bure ; [translated from the French by Willard Wood]. — English-language ed.
    p. cm.
  French ed. published: Paris : Editions de La Martinière, 2011.
  Includes bibliographical references and index.
  ISBN 978-1-4197-0310-2 (alk. paper)
  1. Saint Laurent, Yves. 2. Fashion designers—France—Paris.
  3. Fashion design—France—Paris—History—20th century.
  I. Bure, Gilles de. II. Title.
  TT505.S24S3813 2012
  746.9'20944361—dc23
                                        2011038224

THE ART OF BOOKS SINCE 1949
115 West 18th Street
New York, NY 10011
www.abramsbooks.com

SAINT LAURENT
rive gauche